Jump Start Your Career
in Technology & IT
in about 100 Pages

Table of Contents

Let's Start !

Introduction

Objective-C is the programming language behind native Apple applications. The language was originally designed in the 1980s as a way to add object-oriented capabilities to the ANSI C programming language, and it has since been used to create everything from command-line tools to Mac programs to mobile apps. You can think of Objective-C as Apple's version of the C# programming language.

However, learning Objective-C is only one aspect of iPhone, iPad, and Mac app development. On top of the language lie a handful of frameworks that provide the tools necessary to build apps for any of these platforms. For example, the UIKit framework defines the basic UI components you see on your iPhone (buttons, lists, images, etc.), while the Core Data framework provides an API for saving and retrieving data from a device. Objective-C is the glue that lets you pull together these tools and assemble them into a useful program.

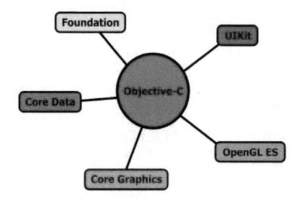

Figure 1: Objective-C pulling together aspects of several frameworks

Objective-C Succinctly is the first installment in a two-part series on Apple app development. In this book, we'll explore the entire Objective-C language using hands-on examples. We'll focus on learning core language concepts by building command-line tools, which means we *won't* be building graphical applications in this book. This lays the foundation for *iOS Succinctly*, which explores the iOS framework underlying iPhone and iPad apps. Both books utilize Xcode, Apple's official integrated development environment.

The Objective-C Language

For developers coming from a C# background, Objective-C retains many of the same workflows and object-oriented concepts. You still write code, compile it into an executable, and, of course, use objects to organize your application. Objective-C provides standard object-oriented constructs like interfaces, classes, class/instance methods, and accessors. That said, there are a few important differences between Objective-C and languages like C++ and C#.

The first thing you'll notice is that Objective-C uses a completely different syntax for communicating between objects. For example, compare the *method calling* syntax of C# to the *message sending* syntax of Objective-C:

```
person.sayHello();     // C# method calling.
[person sayHello];     // Objective-C message sending.
```

Instead of calling a method that's bound to an object, Objective-C "sends messages" from object to object using the square bracket notation. For most practical purposes, you can approach message sending as method calling, and we'll use the terms interchangeably unless it leads to confusion.

Second, Objective-C is designed to be a superset of C, meaning it's possible to compile C code with any Objective-C compiler. This also means you can combine Objective-C and C in the same project or even in the same file. In addition, most modern compilers add C++ to the mix, so it's actually possible to mix Objective-C, C++, and C in a single file. This can be very confusing for newcomers to Objective-C, but it also makes the entire C/C++ ecosystem accessible to Mac and iOS apps.

We'll explore these differences and much more throughout *Objective-C Succinctly*.

Sample Code

You will learn more from this book if you recreate the samples using the code provided in the book.

A select set of samples using the code provided in the book is available online. These samples are essential to understanding Objective-C. These samples are available for download from https://bitbucket.org/syncfusion/objective_c_succinctly. Samples that apply to specific sections are mentioned in the section they apply, using the following format:

Included code sample: {name of the sample folder}

Setting Up

There are a number of compilers for Objective-C, but this book will focus on the Xcode IDE, which comes with a compiler, text editor, debugger, interface editor, and everything else you need to create iOS apps in a convenient package. At the time of this writing, Xcode is only available for OS X, so you'll need to be on a Mac before you can run any of the code in this book.

We'll start by walking through the installation of Xcode, and then we'll learn how to create an application and explore some of the prominent features of the IDE.

Installation

Xcode

Everything you need to create great
apps for Mac, iPhone, and iPad.

Figure 2: The Xcode logo in the Mac App Store

Xcode can be downloaded from the Mac App Store. Navigate to the link or search for **Xcode** in the Mac App Store, and then click **Free** in the upper left-hand corner to start the download. The Xcode app is rather large, so it will take at least a few minutes to download. If you're not sure whether the download is working, you can check its status in the **Purchases** tab of the Mac App Store:

Figure 3: The Purchases tab in the Mac App Store

Scroll down to find the Xcode download and you should see a progress bar indicating how far along it is. Once the download has completed, the installation should be straightforward, and you should (hopefully) see a friendly welcome screen when you launch the program.

Figure 4: The Xcode welcome screen

Creating an Application

Our first Objective-C application will be a simple command-line "Hello, World!" program. To create the Xcode project, click **Create a new Xcode project** in the welcome screen. As an alternative, you can also select **File > New > Project**.... This gives you the opportunity to select a project template. As you can see, templates are categorized as either iOS apps or Mac OS X apps. In the second part of this series, we'll work with several of the iOS templates, but for now, let's stick to the simple **Command Line Tool** template under **Mac OS X > Application**:

Figure 5: Mac OS X template categories and Command Line Tool template icon

Next, you should be presented with some configuration options for your new project. For the **Product Name**, use **HelloObjectiveC**. If you were planning on distributing this program, you would need to acquire a Company Identifier by registering as a developer with Apple, but since this is a personal project, you can use **edu.self**. This serves as a unique namespace for the application. For **Type**, select **Foundation** (more on this later), and be sure to select the **Use Automatic Reference Counting** check box since we don't want to manually manage memory. Your final configuration options should look like the following:

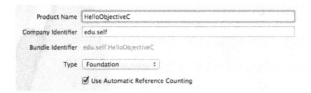

Figure 6: Configuration options for our new project

Finally, you should be able to select a location to save your project. Save it wherever you like, but deselect the **Source Control** option at the bottom of the window. This would initialize a Git repository in your project folder, but we're working with such a small project that we don't need to worry about revision control.

Figure 7: Deselecting the Source Control option

After selecting a location for the project and clicking **Create**, Xcode creates a new folder called **HelloObjectiveC**. In it, you should find *another* **HelloObjectiveC** folder containing the project files, along with a **HelloObjectiveC.xcodeproj** folder; however, the latter acts more like a file than a folder. **HelloObjectiveC.xcodeproj** defines the metadata for your application, as well as local configuration settings for the IDE.

The only file that you actually *need* in a **.xcodeproj** folder is the **project.pbxproj** file, which contains build settings and other project-related information. That is to say, if your project was under source control, **project.pbxproj** is the only file in **HelloObjectiveC.xcodeproj** that would need to be under version control.

Double-clicking the **HelloObjectiveC.xcodeproj** folder will launch Xcode and open the project.

Getting to Know the Xcode IDE

Xcode is a large application with many capabilities, and it has a correspondingly complex interface. It's worth taking some time to familiarize yourself with the various UI components highlighted in the following screenshot.

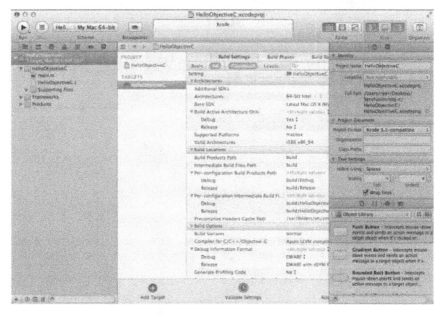

Figure 8: Main components of the Xcode IDE

As you can see, the Xcode interface is split into three main windows: a project navigator (blue), an editor/work area (yellow), and a utilities area (purple). The navigator lets you select files, find code breaks, and debug your program. The editor is where you'll do the bulk of your work—it's where you edit code and, for graphical applications, where you design your user interfaces and control the flow of an app. But again, for *Objective-C Succinctly*, we won't need any of the interface editing tools. Finally, the utilities area lets you define options for the selected component (e.g., the build targets associated with a particular file).

You can control which of these windows are visible using the view selector (green) in the upper right corner; however, it's not possible to hide the work area. Clicking the center button in the view selector will display an output window where we can see log data for our application.

Editing Files

Our command-line template comes with a single Objective-C file, **main.m**. The .m extension is used for files that only contain Objective-C code, and the .mm extension is for files with a mix of Objective-C and C, Objective-C and C++, or a combination of all three. To edit **main.m**, select it in the navigator panel, and you should see the following code appear in the editor window:

```
//
// main.m
// HelloObjectiveC
//
// Created by Ryan Hodson on 8/21/12.
// Copyright (c) 2012 __MyCompanyName__. All rights reserved.
#import <Foundation/Foundation.h>

int main(int argc, const char * argv[])
{

    @autoreleasepool {

        // Insert code here...
        NSLog(@"Hello, World!");

    }
    return 0;
}
```

The next chapter provides an in-depth explanation of this code, but for now, the only important thing is the **NSLog()** function, which outputs a string to the console. Also notice that Objective-C strings are prefixed with an **@** symbol (as are most constructs that are exclusive to Objective-C), and they must be double-quoted.

Compiling Code

Included code sample: HelloObjectiveC

To compile this code and run the resulting executable, simply click the **Run** button in the upper-left corner of the IDE. Alternatively, you can select **Product** > **Run** in the main menu bar, or use the Cmd+R keyboard shortcut. This should open the output panel at the bottom of the screen with a "Hello, World!" message:

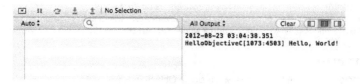

Figure 9: HelloObjectiveC log output

Summary

And those are the basics of installing the Xcode IDE and using it to create and compile an Objective-C project. We didn't do any coding, but hopefully you're feeling more comfortable with the Xcode interface and are at least able to navigate your way through a project's files. In the next chapter, we'll start actually writing Objective-C code, defining classes, instantiating objects, and sending messages to them.

Chapter 1 Hello, Objective-C

This chapter is designed to help you acclimate to Objective-C programming style. By the end of this chapter, you will be able to instantiate objects, create and call methods, and declare properties. Remember that the goal is to provide a very brief survey of the major object-oriented aspects of Objective-C, not a detailed description of each component. Later chapters fill in many of the conceptual details omitted from this chapter.

Creating a Class

Included code sample: HelloObjectiveC With Class

Let's dive right in and create a new Objective-C file. In the Xcode IDE, navigate to **File > New > File...** or use the Cmd+N shortcut to add a file to your project. The next dialog lets you select which kind of file you would like to create. Under the **Cocoa Touch** category, select **Objective-C class**.

Figure 10: The Objective-C class icon

You're given an opportunity to specify a name for your new class. Let's call our class `Person`. For the parent class, use `NSObject`, which is the top-level object from which all Objective-C classes inherit.

Figure 11: Defining a new Person class

Clicking **Next** will open a file browser and ask you to enter a **Group** for your class, as well as a **Target**. Use the default **Group**, which should be **HelloObjectiveC**. Groups are an Xcode-specific mechanism for grouping similar files, but they *aren't* implemented on the file level. Our new class will appear in the same folder as the rest of the project files, regardless of what group it's in. For **Targets**, make sure **HelloObjectiveC** is selected. This ensures the new class is compiled whenever we build the HelloObjectiveC target.

Figure 12: Selecting build targets for the new class

Finally, click **Create** to create the class. In the Xcode file navigator, you should now find two new classes: **Person.h** and **Person.m**. Just like the C programming language, Objective-C uses **.h** as the extension for header files, which contain the interface for a particular function or class—this is not to be confused with a C# interface, which is called a **protocol** in Objective-C. The **.m** file is the corresponding implementation for the `Person` class.

Separating a class' interface from its implementation makes it possible to hide implementation details from third-party objects. Other files that need to interact with the class import the *header* file—never the *implementation* file. This provides the abstract definition necessary to call methods and access properties while being completely independent of the class' implementation.

Components of a Class

In the project navigator, select **Person.h** to open it in the editor panel. You should see the following Objective-C code:

```
#import <Foundation/Foundation.h>

@interface Person : NSObject

@end
```

The **#import** directive includes another file in the current context. Including a header file gives us access to all of the classes and functions it defines. In this case, we included the Foundation framework. The Foundation framework defines the basic constructs of the Objective-C language—things like strings, arrays, dictionaries, etc.—so it's a necessary part of virtually every Objective-C program.

The **@interface** directive begins an interface for a class. Next comes the class name, `Person`, followed by a colon and the parent class, **NSObject**. As noted earlier, **NSObject** is the top-level object in Objective-C. It contains the necessary methods for creating and destroying instances, along with some other useful functionality shared by all objects.

Any methods or properties would be declared before the **@end** directive, but right now, **Person.h** is an empty interface. We'll change that in a minute, but first let's take a quick glance at the implementation file, **Person.m**:

```
#import "Person.h"
```

```
@implementation Person

@end
```

This looks a lot like the header file, but it includes the `Person.h` header. Implementation files *must* include their associated header, otherwise they won't be able to find the class that they're trying to implement.

Also notice that this `#import` directive uses quotation marks instead of angled brackets. Quotation marks should be used to import *local* headers, while brackets indicate *global* headers. Global headers reside outside of the project and are linked to the compiler during the build process. Apple's standard frameworks are always included in angled brackets, whereas your project files should be imported with quotation marks.

And of course, the **.m** file uses the `@implementation` directive instead of `@interface`. Note that you *don't* have to specify the parent class here, since this information is already contained in the header.

Defining Methods

Next, we'll add a method declaration to the `Person` class. Remember that this is a two-step process: first we have to add it to the interface, and then the implementation. So, change **Person.h** to the following:

```
#import <Foundation/Foundation.h>

@interface Person : NSObject

- (void)sayHello;

@end
```

As you can see, instance methods are declared with a hyphen, the return type in parentheses (**void**), followed by the method name and a semicolon. Now that we have that in the interface, switch over to **Person.m** to define the implementation. Note that Xcode added a little yellow triangle next to the `@implementation` line. If you click it, you'll find a warning message that says *Incomplete implementation*. This is one of Xcode's numerous debugging features. Let's fix that issue by changing **Person.m** to the following:

```
#import "Person.h"

@implementation Person

- (void)sayHello {
    NSLog(@"Hello, my name is HAL.");
```

```
}
@end
```

Like the interface declaration, the implementation for an instance method begins with a hyphen, the return type, and the function name. The implementation itself is defined in the curly braces after the method name, just like a C# method. For **sayHello**, we just output a message to the console using **NSLog()**.

As you type, Xcode presents some autocompletion options, and it also should have closed your curly braces for you. These behaviors can be changed by navigating to **Xcode > Preferences...** in the menu bar and clicking the **Text Editing** icon.

Instantiating Objects

Let's try instantiating our **Person** class and calling our new **sayHello** method. Remember that like any C program, **main()** is the entry point into our *HelloObjectiveC* application. So, back in **main.m**, change **NSLog(@"Hello, World!");** to the following:

```
#import <Foundation/Foundation.h>
#import "Person.h"

int main(int argc, const char * argv[]) {
    @autoreleasepool {

        Person *somePerson = [[Person alloc] init];

    }
    return 0;
}
```

The **Person *somePerson** expression declares a variable called **somePerson** and tells the compiler that it's going to hold an instance of the **Person** class. The asterisk next to the variable name indicates that it's a **pointer**, which is the most common way to reference objects in Objective-C. We'll discuss pointers in more detail down the road.

Next, the **[[Person alloc] init]** code creates a new instance of the **Person** class. The square bracket notation may take some getting used to, but it's conceptually the same as the parentheses used for method calls in C# and other Simula-style languages. The previous code sample is equivalent to the following in C#:

```
Person somePerson = new Person();
somePerson.init();
```

The **[Person alloc]** call allocates the memory required for the new instance, and the **init** call is used to execute any kind of custom initialization code. Note that there are no "constructor methods" in Objective-C as there are in C# or C++—you must manually call the the **init** method (or some variant thereof) to set up your object. As a result, virtually all object creation in Objective-C is a two-step process: allocate, and then initialize. You will see this pattern quite often in Objective-C programs.

Calling Methods

Now that we have an object to work with, we can call our **sayHello** method. Note that the correct terminology in Objective-C is "sending a message," not "calling a method," but for our purposes, we can treat them as synonymous. Add the following line to **main.m**:

```
[somePerson sayHello];
```

Just like the **alloc/init** methods in the previous example, custom method invocation uses square brackets. Again, this is the same as executing **somePerson.sayHello()** in C#. Running your program should display **Hello, my name is HAL.** in the Xcode output panel:

Figure 13: Output generated from the sayHello method

Adding Method Parameters

Aside from the square brackets, Objective-C's method naming conventions are one of the biggest adjustments for developers coming from C#, C++, Java, Python, or pretty much any other language that's not Smalltalk. Objective-C method names are designed to be as descriptive as possible. The idea is to define a method in such a way that reading it aloud literally tells you what it does.

As an example, let's add a **name** parameter to our **sayHello** method. First, we need to update the method declaration in the header (**Person.h**):

```
- (void)sayHelloToName:(NSString *)aName;
```

Adding a parameter actually *changed the name of the function*—the parameter is not an isolated entity as it is in C# (e.g., **sayHello(name)**). The **(NSString *)** portion defines the data type of the parameter, and **aName** is the actual variable that can be accessed in the implementation code, which we'll define now. Change **sayHello** in **Person.m** to the code sample that follows. Xcode should autocomplete the new method name when you start typing it.

```
- (void)sayHelloToName:(NSString *)aName {
    NSLog(@"Hello %@, my name is HAL.", aName);
}
```

```
}
```

This new **NSLog()** configuration uses a format string to add the **aName** argument to the output. We'll cover **NSLog()** in more detail in the next chapter, but for now all you need to know is that it replaces **%@** in the format string with **aName**. This is roughly equivalent to **String.Format()** in C#.

Calling the parameter **aName** might seem redundant with **sayHelloToName**, but it makes more sense when you read the method as it would be invoked. In **main.m**, change the **sayHello** call to:

```
[somePerson sayHelloToName:@"Bill"];
```

Now, you should be able to run your program and see **Hello Bill, my name is HAL.** in the output panel. As you can see, Objective-C method names are verbose, but quite informative. Unlike the C#-style **sayHello(name)** invocation, Objective-C makes it very hard to accidentally pass the wrong value to a method. Of course, the trade-off is that method names are long, but that's why Xcode provides such a convenient autocompletion feature. We'll see many more verbose (and more practical) examples of Objective-C method names throughout this book.

Defining Properties

Included code sample: With Properties

As with any object-oriented language, Objective-C methods are a means to manipulate the internal state of an object. This state is typically represented as a set of properties attached to an object. For example, we can add a **name** property to our **Person** interface to store each instance's name dynamically:

```
@property (copy) NSString *name;
```

The **@property** declaration begins a new property, the **(copy)** tuple specifies the behavior of the property, and **NSString *name** defines a property called **name** that holds a string value. Typically, property declarations are placed before method declarations, but as long as it's somewhere between **@interface** and **@end** in **Person.h**, you'll be fine.

Using **@property** instead of private attributes gives you access to the **@synthesize** directive in the implementation file. It lets you automatically create accessor methods for the associated property. For example, in **Person.m**, add the following (again, property implementations usually come before method implementations):

```
@synthesize name = _name;
```

@synthesize is a convenience directive that tells the compiler to generate getter and setter methods for the property. The part after the = sign is used as the instance variable (i.e. private member) for the property, which means we can use **_name** to access the name property inside of **Person.m**. For example, try changing the **sayHelloToName** method to:

```
- (void)sayHelloToName:(NSString *)aName {
    NSLog(@"Hello %@, my name is %@.", aName, _name);
}
```

By default, the getter method name is the same as the property name, and the setter has **set** prepended to the capitalized property name. So, we can dynamically set our **Person** object's name by changing **main.m** to the following:

```
Person *somePerson = [[Person alloc] init];
[somePerson setName:@"HAL 9000"];
[somePerson sayHelloToName:@"Bill"];
```

Running your program should now produce **Hello Bill, my name is HAL 9000**.

Summary

This chapter presented the basic components of an Objective-C class. We learned how to separate classes into interface (**.h**) and implementation files (**.m**), instantiate objects, define and call methods, and declare properties. Hopefully, you're feeling a little bit more comfortable with Objective-C's square bracket notation and other syntactic quirks.

Remember that this chapter was designed to be a quick introduction to Objective-C's OOP constructs, not an in-depth discussion of each component. In the upcoming chapters, we'll take a more detailed look at data types, property declarations, method definitions, as well as the common design patterns of Objective-C programs.

Chapter 2 Data Types

Objective-C has two categories of data types. First, remember that Objective-C is a superset of C, so you have access to all of the native C data types like char, int, float, etc. Objective-C also defines a few of its own low-level types, including a Boolean type. Let's call all of these "primitive data types."

Second, Objective-C provides several high-level data structures like strings, arrays, dictionaries, and dates. These high-level data types are implemented as Objective-C objects, so you'll see many of the same object-oriented constructs from the previous chapter. Since these are all defined in the Foundation framework, we'll call them "foundation data structures."

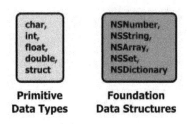

Figure 14: Our two categories of data types

This chapter covers both primitive data types and the most important foundation data structures. By the end of this chapter, you should have a solid grasp of every data structure you could possibly need for your Objective-C programs.

Displaying Values

In addition to data types, we'll also learn a lot more about NSLog() string formatting in this chapter. This will let us display variables of all sorts in the Xcode console, which is an indispensable skill for debugging applications.

As we saw in the previous chapter, NSLog() can be called with a **format string.** Inside of the format string, you use the % symbol to designate placeholder values, and NSLog() will fill them in with values passed as additional parameters. For example, the %@ in the following code is replaced with the **aName** variable:

```
NSLog(@"Hello %@, my name is HAL.", aName);
```

The %@ is used as a placeholder for *objects* (Objective-C strings are implemented as objects), but primitive data types use their own format specifiers, which will be covered in their respective sections.

Primitive Data Types

The first half of this chapter looks at the native Objective-C data types and discusses how to display them using **NSLog()** format strings. The size of the data types presented in this section is system-dependent—the only way to truly know how big your data types are is to use the **sizeof()** function. For example, you can check the size of a **char** with the following:

```
NSLog(@"%lu", sizeof(char));
```

This should output **1**, which means that **char** takes up 1 byte of memory. The **%lu** placeholder is for unsigned long integers (discussed in more detail later), which is the return type for **sizeof()**. Upcoming sections discuss the most common sizes for Objective-C data types, but remember that this may differ from your system.

Booleans

Objective-C programs use the **BOOL** data type to store Boolean values. Objective-C also defines its own true and false keywords, which are **YES** and **NO**, respectively. To display **BOOL** values via **NSLog()**, use **%i** in the format string:

```
BOOL isHuman = NO;
NSLog(@"It's alive: %i", isHuman);
```

The **%i** specifier is used to display integers, so this should output **It's alive: 0**.

Technically, **BOOL** is a macro for the **signed char** type (discussed in the next section). This means that **BOOL** variables can store many more values than just **YES** and **NO**, which are actually macros for **1** and **0**, respectively. However, most developers will never use this extra functionality, since it can be a source of frustrating bugs in conditional statements:

```
BOOL isHuman = 127;
if (isHuman) {
    // This will execute.
    NSLog(@"isHuman is TRUE");
}
if (isHuman == YES) {
    // But this *won't* execute.
    NSLog(@"isHuman is YES");
}
```

Any value greater than **0** will evaluate to true, so the first condition will execute, but the second will not because **127 != 1**. Depending on how you're using your **BOOL** variables, this may or may not be a desirable distinction.

Chars

Objective-C uses the same `char` data type as ANSI C. It denotes a single-byte signed integer, and can be used to store values between -128 and 127 or an ASCII character. To display a `char` as an integer, just use the generic %i specifier introduced in the previous code sample. To format it as an ASCII character, use %c:

```
char letter = 'z';
NSLog(@"The ASCII letter %c is actually the number %i", letter, letter);
```

As with all integer data types, it's possible to allocate an *unsigned* `char`, which can record values from 0 to 255. Instead of the %i specifier, you should use %u as a placeholder for unsigned integers:

```
unsigned char tinyInt = 255;
NSLog(@"The unsigned char is: %u", tinyInt);
```

Short Integers

Short integers are 2-byte signed integers and should be used for values between -32768 and 32767. To display them with `NSLog()`, use the %hi specifier (the h is a "modifier" for the same %i used in the previous two sections). For example:

```
short int littleInt = 27000;
NSLog(@"The short int is: %hi", littleInt);
```

Unsigned shorts can be created the same way as unsigned chars and can hold up to 65535. Again, the u in %hu is the same one in %u for generic unsigned integers:

```
unsigned short int ulittleInt = 42000;
NSLog(@"The unsigned short integer is: %hu", ulittleInt);
```

"Normal" Integers

Next on the list is `int`, which is a 4-byte integer on most systems. Again, remember that data type size is system-dependent—the only way to know for sure how big your data types are is to use the `sizeof()` function:

```
NSLog(@"%lu", sizeof(int));
```

If your `int` type is indeed 4 bytes, it can hold values between -2147483648 and 2147483647.

```
int normalInt = 1234567890;
```

```
NSLog(@"The normal integer is: %i", normalInt);
```

This also means that the unsigned version can record **0–4294967295**.

Long Integers

If **int** isn't big enough to meet your needs, you can move up to the **long int** data type, which is 8 bytes on most modern systems. This is large enough to represent values between **-9223372036854775808** and **9223372036854775807**. Long integers can be displayed via **NSLog()** by prepending the letter **l** to the **%i** or **%u** specifiers, as shown in the following code:

```
long int bigInt = 9223372036854775807;
NSLog(@"The big integer is: %li", bigInt);

unsigned long int uBigInt = 18446744073709551615;
NSLog(@"The even bigger integer is: %lu", uBigInt);
```

18446744073709551615 is the maximum value for the unsigned version, which is hopefully the largest integer you'll ever need to store.

The idea behind having so many integer data types is to give developers the power to balance their program's memory footprint versus its numerical capacity.

Floats

Objective-C programs can use the **float** type for representing 4-byte floating point numbers. Literal values should be suffixed with **f** to mark the value as single precision instead of a **double** (discussed in the next section). Use the **%f** specifier to output floats with **NSLog()**:

```
float someRealNumber = 0.42f;
NSLog(@"The floating-point number is: %f", someRealNumber);
```

You can also specify the output format for the float itself by including a decimal before the **f**. For example, **%5.3f** will display 3 digits after the decimal and pad the result so there are 5 places total (useful for aligning the decimal point when listing values).

While floating-point values have a much larger range than their fixed-point counterparts, it's important to remember that they are intrinsically *not precise*. Careful consideration must be paid to comparing floating-point values, and they should never be used to record precision-sensitive data (e.g., money). For representing fixed-point values in Objective-C, please see **NSDecimalNumber** in the the <u>Foundation Data Structures</u> section.

Doubles

The **double** data type is a double-precision floating-point number. For the most part, you can treat it as a more accurate version of **float**. You can use the same **%f** specifier for displaying **doubles** in **NSLog()**, but you don't need to append **f** to literal values:

```
double anotherRealNumber = 0.42;
NSLog(@"The floating-point number is: %5.3f", anotherRealNumber);
```

Structs

Objective-C also provides access to C structs, which can be used to define custom data structures. For example, if you're working on a graphics program and interact with many 2-dimensional points, it's convenient to wrap them in a custom type:

```
typedef struct {
    float x;
    float y;
} Point2D;
```

The **typedef** keyword tells the compiler we're defining a new data type, **struct** creates the actual data structure, which comprises the variables **x** and **y**, and finally, **Point2D** is the name of the new data type. After declaring this **struct**, you can use **Point2D** just like you would use any of the built-in types. For instance, the following snippet creates the point **(10.0, 0.5)** and displays it using our existing **NSLog()** format specifiers.

```
Point2D p1 = {10.0f, 0.5f};
NSLog(@"The point is at: (%.1f, %.1f)", p1.x, p1.y);
```

The **{10.0f, 0.5f}** notation is called a compound literal, and it can be used to initialize a **struct**. After initialization, you can also assign new values to a **struct**'s properties with the = operator:

```
p1.x = -2.5f;
p1.y = 2.5f;
```

Structures are important for performance-intensive applications, but they sometimes prove difficult to integrate with the high-level Foundation data structures. Unless you're working with 3-D graphics or some other CPU-heavy application, you're usually better off storing custom data structures in a full-fledged class instead of a **struct**.

Arrays

While Objective-C provides its own object-oriented array data types, it still gives you access to the low-level arrays specified by ANSI C. C arrays are a contiguous block of memory allocated when they're declared, and all of their elements must be of the same type. Unlike C# arrays, this means you need to define an array's length when it's declared, and you can't assign another array to it after it's been initialized.

Because there is no way for a program to automatically determine how many elements are in an array, there is no convenient **NSLog()** format specifier for displaying native arrays. Instead, we're stuck with manually looping through each element and calling a separate NSLog(). For example, the following code creates and displays an array of 5 integers:

```
int someValues[5] = {15, 32, 49, 90, 14};
for (int i=0; i<5; i++) {
    NSLog(@"The value at index %i is: %i", i, someValues[i]);
}
```

As you can see, C arrays look much like atomic variables, except you have to provide their length in square brackets ([5]). They can be initialized with the same compound literal syntax as structs, but all the values must be of the same type. Individual elements can be accessed by passing the item number in square brackets, which is common in most programming languages. In addition, you can access elements via pointers.

Pointers

Pointers provide a low-level way to directly access memory addresses in a C program. And, since C arrays are just contiguous blocks of memory, pointers are a natural way to interact with items in an array. In fact, the variable holding a native array is actually a pointer to the first element in the array.

Pointers are created by prefixing the variable name with an asterisk (*). For example, we can create a second reference to the first element in the someValues array with the following code:

```
int someValues[5] = {15, 32, 49, 90, 14};
int *pointer = someValues;
```

Instead of storing an int value, the *pointer variable *points* to the memory address containing the value. This can be visualized as the following:

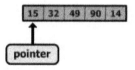

Figure 15: Pointer to the first element of an array

To get the underlying value out of the memory address, we need to **dereference** the pointer using the asterisk operator, like so:

```
NSLog(@"The first value is: %i", *pointer);
```

This should display **15** in your output panel, since that is the value stored in the memory address pointed to by the **pointer** variable. So far, this is just a very confusing way to access a normal (non-pointer) **int** variable. However, things get much more interesting when you start *moving* pointers around with the **++** and -- operators. For example, we can increment the pointer to the next memory address as follows:

```
pointer++;
NSLog(@"The next value is: %i", *pointer);
```

Since an array is a contiguous block of memory, the pointer will now rest at the address of the second element of the array. As a result, the **NSLog()** call should display **32** instead of **15**. This can be visualized as the following:

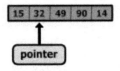

Figure 16: Incrementing the pointer to the second element of an array

Pointers provide an alternative way to iterate through an array. Instead of accessing items via the square brackets (e.g., **someValues[i]**), you can simply increment the pointer and dereference it to get the next value:

```
for (int i=0; i<5; i++) {
    pointer++;
    NSLog(@"The value at index %i is: %i", i, *pointer);
}
```

Pointers have innumerable uses in high-performance applications, but in reality, you probably won't need to use pointers with native arrays unless you're building a data-intensive application that is seriously concerned with speed.

However, pointers are still very important to Objective-C programs because *every* object is referenced through a pointer. This is why all of the data structures in the upcoming Foundation Data Structures section are declared as pointers (e.g., **NSNumber *someNumber**, not **NSNumber someNumber**).

Void

The **void** type represents the absence of a value. Instead of typing variables, **void** is used with functions and methods that don't return a value. For example, the **sayHello** method from the previous chapter didn't return anything, and it was thus defined with the **void** data type:

```
- (void)sayHello;
```

nil and NULL

The `nil` and `NULL` keywords are both used to represent empty pointers. This is useful for explicitly stating that a variable doesn't contain anything, rather than leaving it as a pointer to its most recent memory address.

There is, however, a strict distinction between the two. The `nil` constant should only be used as an empty value for Objective-C objects—it should *not* be used to for native C-style pointers (e.g., `int *somePointer`). `NULL` can be used for either primitive pointers or Objective-C object pointers, though `nil` is the preferred choice.

Primitive Data Type Summary

The first half of this chapter introduced the primitive data types available to Objective-C programmers. We also took a brief look at pointers and the `nil` and `NULL` keywords.

It's important to remember that the value stored in a variable is completely independent from how it's interpreted. `unsigned int`s can be interpreted as `signed int`s without changing the variable in any way. That's why it's so important to make sure you're using the right format string in `NSLog()`. Otherwise, you'll be left wondering why your unsigned variables look like they're storing negative numbers. As we'll see in the next section, this isn't as much of a problem with object-oriented data types.

The remainder of this chapter focuses on the Foundation framework, which defines several object-oriented data structures that all Objective-C developers should be familiar with.

Foundation Data Structures

Primitive data types are essential to any Objective-C program, but it's often tedious to work on such a low level. The Foundation framework abstracts these native types into high-level, object-oriented tools, which lets you focus on how your application works instead of how to store your data.

The data structures that follow are common to most high-level programming languages, but since it's Objective-C, they have unique method names for manipulating the data they contain. The goal of this section is to introduce you to the most important aspects of the core classes defined in the Foundation framework, rather than to provide a comprehensive API reference. If you're looking for the latter, please visit the Foundation Framework Reference.

NSNumber

NSNumber is a generic container for numeric types (i.e. `BOOL`, `char`, `short`, `int`, `long`, `float`, and `double`). It lets you take one of the primitive types discussed earlier in this chapter and interact with it in an object-oriented fashion. This is called **boxing**, and it's an essential tool for integrating Objective-C with C and C++ libraries.

`NSNumber` provides several convenient methods to convert to and from primitive values. For example, you can store an integer in `NSNumber` with the following:

```
int someInteger = -27;
NSNumber *someNumber = [NSNumber numberWithInt:someInteger];
```

Likewise, **floats** can be created with **numberWithFloat:**, **doubles** can be created with
numberWithDouble:, **BOOLs** can be created with **numberWithBool:**, etc., The recorded value
can be accessed with the corresponding accessor method:

```
NSLog(@"The stored number is: %i", [someNumber intValue]);
```

Accessors for other primitives follow the same pattern: **floatValue**, **doubleValue**, **boolValue**, etc.

Remember that the **%@** specifier is used as a placeholder for objects. Most classes in the
Foundation framework define their own display formats. **NSNumber** will simply display its stored
value, so the following format string will output the exact same thing as the previous snippet.
Not having to figure out which specifier to use is one of the convenient perks of using **NSNumber**.

```
NSLog(@"The stored number is: %@", someNumber);
```

Note that **NSNumber** is an immutable type, so you'll have to create a new instance if you need to
change the stored value. This may seem like a lot of overhead, but compared to everything else
going on in an Objective-C program, it's not actually that much of a performance hit. Of course,
if it becomes a problem, you can always fall back to the native C primitives.

One of the other perks of **NSNumber** is the ability to set a variable to **nil** to indicate an empty
value. There is no way to do this with primitive numerical values.

NSDecimalNumber

The NSDecimalNumber class is Objective-C's fixed-point class. It can represent much more
precise numbers than **float** or **double**, and is thus the preferred way to represent money or
other precision-sensitive data. The easiest way to create an **NSDecimalNumber** is to use the
decimalNumberWithString: method, like so:

```
NSDecimalNumber *subtotal = [NSDecimalNumber
                            decimalNumberWithString:@"10.99"];
```

Since **NSDecimalNumber** uses more precise arithmetic algorithms than floating-point numbers,
you can't use the standard +,-,*, or / operators. Instead, **NSDecimalNumber** provides its own
methods for all of these operations:

- - **decimalNumberByAdding:(NSDecimalNumber *)aNumber**
- - **decimalNumberBySubtracting:(NSDecimalNumber *)aNumber**
- - **decimalNumberByMultiplyingBy:(NSDecimalNumber *)aNumber**
- - **decimalNumberByDividingBy:(NSDecimalNumber *)aNumber**

Like **NSNumber**, **NSDecimalNumber** is an immutable type, so all of these methods return a new instance of **NSDecimalNumber**. For example, the next snippet multiplies a product's price by a discount percentage:

```
NSDecimalNumber *subtotal = [NSDecimalNumber
                        decimalNumberWithString:@"10.99"];
NSDecimalNumber *discount = [NSDecimalNumber
                        decimalNumberWithString:@".25"];
NSDecimalNumber *total = [subtotal decimalNumberByMultiplyingBy:discount];
NSLog(@"The product costs: $%@", total);
```

However, if you run this code sample, you'll notice that it outputs a few extra places after the decimal. Fortunately, **NSDecimalNumber** provides detailed options for configuring its rounding behavior. This is the primary reason to use **NSDecimalNumber** over the primitive **float** or **double** data types. To define your rounding behavior, create an instance of **NSDecimalNumberHandler** with your desired parameters, and then pass it to **NSDecimalNumber**'s arithmetic operations via the **withBehavior** parameter. The following configuration is useful for working with currencies:

```
NSDecimalNumberHandler *roundUp = [NSDecimalNumberHandler
    decimalNumberHandlerWithRoundingMode:NSRoundUp
                        scale:2
                raiseOnExactness:NO
                raiseOnOverflow:NO
                raiseOnUnderflow:NO
            raiseOnDivideByZero:YES];

NSDecimalNumber *roundedTotal = [subtotal
    decimalNumberByMultiplyingBy:discount
                withBehavior:roundUp];

NSLog(@"The product costs: $%@", roundedTotal);
```

The **NSRoundUp** argument tells **NSDecimalNumber** operations to round up (the other options are **NSRoundPlain**, **NSRoundDown**, and **NSRoundBankers**). Next, the **scale** parameter defines the maximum number of digits after the decimal point (note that negative values will start removing significant figures to the left of the decimal point). The rest of the parameters define the exception handling behavior of **NSDecimalNumber** operations. In this case, we're telling it to ignore everything that could go wrong unless we try to divide by zero. Together, these arguments make sure that we always have two decimals in our currency values and that they are always rounded up.

Generally, an instance of **NSDecimalNumber** is only useful for interacting with other **NSDecimalNumber** objects, but you may occasionally need to convert them to another data type:

```
double totalAsDouble = [roundedTotal doubleValue];
NSString *totalAsString = [roundedTotal stringValue];
```

The **stringValue** method is particularly useful for exporting values to a database or some other persistent storage (**NSDecimalNumber** should never be stored as a **double** unless you really don't care about loss of precision). It's also worth mentioning that the Core Data framework does provide a native storage mechanism for **NSDecimalNumber**, although that's outside the scope of this book.

NSString

NSString is the immutable string class used by the vast majority of Objective-C programs. We've already seen it in action in the Hello, Objective-C chapter, but let's take a closer look at some of its methods. At heart, **NSString** is a glorified C array of integers representing characters. Its two most basic methods are:

- `-(NSUInteger)length` – Return the number of characters in the string.

- `-(unichar)characterAtIndex:(NSUInteger)theIndex` – Return the character at **theIndex**.

These two methods make it possible to iterate through individual characters in a string. For example:

```
NSString *quote = @"Open the pod bay doors, HAL.";
for (int i=0; i<[quote length]; i++) {
    NSLog(@"%c", [quote characterAtIndex:i]);
}
```

Yet the real power of **NSString** comes in its higher-level functionality. Some of the most common methods are described in the following list, but keep in mind that this list is far from complete.

- `+(id)stringWithFormat:(NSString *)format ...` – Create a string using the same placeholder format as **NSLog()**.

- `-(NSString *)stringByAppendingString:(NSString *)aString` – Append a string to the receiving object.

- `-(NSString *)stringByAppendingFormat:(NSString *)format ...` – Append a string using the same placeholder format as **NSLog()**.

- `-(NSString *)lowercaseString` – Return the lowercase representation of the receiving string.

- `-(NSString *)substringWithRange:(NSRange)aRange` – Return a substring residing in **aRange** (see following example for usage).

- `-(NSRange)rangeOfString:(NSString *)aString` – Search for **aString** in the receiving string and return the location and length of the result as an **NSRange** (see following example for usage).

- **-(NSString *)stringByReplacingOccurancesOfString:(NSString *)target withString:(NSString *)replacement** – Replace all occurrences of **target** with **replacement**.

This last method is a good example of how the verbose nature of Objective-C method names makes programs self-documenting. It's long to type, but no one will mistake what you are trying to accomplish with this method. The following example demonstrates a few of these higher-level methods and shows you how to use <u>NSRange</u>, which is a struct containing **location** and **length** fields. **NSMakeRange()** is a convenience function defined by the Foundation framework for creating an **NSRange**.

```
NSString *quote = @"Open the pod bay doors, HAL.";
NSRange range = NSMakeRange(4, 18);
NSString *partialQuote = [quote substringWithRange:range];
NSLog(@"%@", partialQuote);

NSString *target = @"HAL";
NSRange result = [quote rangeOfString:target];
NSLog(@"Found %@ at index %lu. It's %lu characters long.",
    target, result.location, result.length);
```

NSString also has the ability to directly read and write the contents of a file, but we'll leave that until the second book of this series, *iOS Succinctly*.

NSMutableString

As you probably could have guessed, **NSMutableString** is the mutable counterpart of **NSString**. A mutable string is one that lets you change individual characters without generating an entirely new string. If you're making many small changes to a string, a mutable string is more efficient, since it changes the characters in place. An immutable string, on the other hand, would have to allocate a *new* string for each change.

NSMutableString is implemented as a subclass of **NSString**, so you have access to all of the **NSString** methods, along with the addition of a few new methods for manipulating the character array in place:

- **-(void)appendString:(NSString *)aString** – Append **aString** to the end of the receiving string.

- **-(void)appendFormat:(NSString *)format ...** – Append a string using the same placeholder format as **NSLog()**.

- **-(void)insertString:(NSString *)aString atIndex (NSUInteger)anIndex** – Insert a string into the specified index.

- **-(void)deleteCharactersInRange:(NSRange)aRange** – Remove characters from the receiving string.

- **-(void)replaceCharactersInRange:(NSRange)aRange withString:(NSString *)aString** – Replace the characters in **aRange** with **aString**.

Note that these methods all have **void** return types, whereas the corresponding **NSString** methods return **NSString** objects. This is indicative of the behavior of mutable strings: nothing needs to be returned, because the characters are manipulated in place.

```
// With immutable strings.
NSString *quote = @"I'm sorry, Dave. I'm afraid I can't do that.";
NSString *newQuote = [quote
                    stringByReplacingCharactersInRange:NSMakeRange(11, 4)
                                        withString:@"Capt'n"];
NSLog(@"%@", newQuote);

// With a mutable string.
NSMutableString *mquote = [NSMutableString stringWithString:quote];
[mquote replaceCharactersInRange:NSMakeRange(11, 4)
                    withString:@"Capt'n"];
NSLog(@"%@", mquote);
```

As you can see in this sample, the basic workflow behind mutable strings is much different than immutable strings. Mutable string methods operate *on the object*, so you can use the same variable over and over, changing its contents on the fly. Immutable string methods need multiple variables; of course, you could assign the new string to the same variable over and over, but new strings would still be generated behind the scenes.

Sometimes it's hard to know when to use immutable versus mutable data types. Mutable strings generally have very specific use cases (e.g., a linguistic parser that operates on tokens), so if you're not sure if you need one, you probably don't. For something like the previous example, an *immutable* string would be more appropriate.

NSArray

Arrays are ordered collections of objects that let you maintain and sort lists of data. Like **NSString**, **NSArray** is immutable, so its contents cannot be changed without requesting an entirely new array. The most important **NSArray** methods are shown in the following list. Once again, this is merely a survey, not a comprehensive overview:

- **+(id)arrayWithObjects:(id)firstObject, ...** – Create a new array by passing in a list of objects.

- **-(NSUInteger)count** – Return the number of elements in the array.

- **-(id)objectAtIndex:(NSUInteger)anIndex** – Return the element in the array at index **anIndex**.

- **-(BOOL)containsObject:(id)anObject** – Return whether or not **anObject** is an element of the array.

- **-(NSUInteger)indexOfObject:(id)anObject** – Return the index of the first occurrence of **anObject** in the array. If the object is not in the array, return the **NSNotFound** constant.

- `-(NSArray *)sortedArrayUsingFunction:(NSInteger (*)(id, id, void *))compareFunction context:(void *)context` – Sort an array by comparing objects with a user-defined function (see the second example that follows for usage).

Note that all of these methods use the generic object type **id** for their arguments. Consequently, **NSArray** can *only* handle objects—it *cannot* be used with primitive data types. The practical function of classes like **NSNumber** should now be much clearer: they facilitate boxing. That is, they make it possible to use **char**, **int**, **float**, etc., with **NSArray** by wrapping them in an object-oriented container. For example, the following snippet shows how you can use **NSArray** to manage a list of **float** values:

```
NSNumber *n1 = [NSNumber numberWithFloat:22.5f];
NSNumber *n2 = [NSNumber numberWithFloat:8.0f];
NSNumber *n3 = [NSNumber numberWithFloat:-2.9f];
NSNumber *n4 = [NSNumber numberWithFloat:13.1f];
NSArray *numbers = [NSArray arrayWithObjects:n1, n2, n3, n4, nil];
NSLog(@"%@", numbers);
```

Compared to primitive C arrays, **NSArray** provides plenty of high-level functionality, but of course, it comes at a cost. Boxing can be an expensive operation for high-performance applications. Imagine a graphics program using tens of thousands of **floats** to represent vertices in 3-D space. Creating that many **NSNumber** objects just for the sake of **NSArray** compatibility is not an efficient use of memory or CPU cycles. In that kind situation, you're probably better off sticking with native C arrays and directly working with primitive data types.

The signature for the **sortedArrayUsingFunction:** method may look intimidating, but it's actually a relatively straightforward way to define a custom sort algorithm for an array. First, you need to define the sort function:

Included code sample: ArraySort

```
NSInteger sortFunction(id item1, id item2, void *context) {
    float number1 = [item1 floatValue];
    float number2 = [item2 floatValue];
    if (number1 < number2) {
        return NSOrderedAscending;
    } else if (number1 > number2) {
        return NSOrderedDescending;
    } else {
        return NSOrderedSame;
    }
}
```

This defines a very simple ascending sort, but it demonstrates the essential components of a sort function. The **item1** and **item2** arguments are the two items currently being compared. Since the values are boxed in an **NSNumber**, we need to pull out the values before comparing them. Then we do the actual comparison, returning **NSOrderedAscending** when **item1** should be placed before **item2**, **NSOrderedDescending** when it should be after **item2**, and returning **NSOrderedSame** when they do not need to be sorted. We can use this sort function like so:

```
int main(int argc, const char * argv[]) {
    @autoreleasepool {

        NSNumber *n1 = [NSNumber numberWithFloat:22.5f];
        NSNumber *n2 = [NSNumber numberWithFloat:8.0f];
        NSNumber *n3 = [NSNumber numberWithFloat:-2.9f];
        NSNumber *n4 = [NSNumber numberWithFloat:13.1f];
        NSArray *numbers = [NSArray arrayWithObjects:n1, n2, n3, n4, nil];
        NSLog(@"%@", numbers);

        NSArray *sortedNumbers = [numbers
                             sortedArrayUsingFunction:sortFunction
                                              context:NULL];
        NSLog(@"%@", sortedNumbers);

    }
    return 0;
}
```

The second **NSLog()** output should show the numbers in ascending order from **-2.9** to **22.5**. **sortedNumbers** is an entirely new array, and the **numbers** variable remains unaltered. They do, however, point to the same instances of **n1**, **n2**, **n3**, and **n4**.

NSMutableArray

NSMutableArray is the mutable counterpart of **NSArray**. It's possible to change items after the array has been allocated and to extend or shrink the array by an arbitrary number of elements. While not as efficient as **NSArray**, the ability to incrementally add or remove items makes **NSMutableArray** a common data structure in Objective-C applications. **NSMutableArray** is a subclass of **NSArray**, so both can be created, accessed, and sorted using the methods in the previous section, but they also provide a few extra methods for manipulating their contents:

- **+(id)arrayWithCapacity:(NSUInteger)numItems** – Create an empty mutable array. The **numItems** argument is used as a size hint, so it should be roughly the number of initial items you plan to store.
- **-(void)addObject:(id)anObject** – Add the given object to the end of the existing array.
- **-(void)insertObject:(id)anObject atIndex:(NSUInteger)anIndex** – Insert the given object into the specified index.
- **-(void)removeObjectAtIndex:(NSUInteger)anIndex** – Remove the object at the specified index.
- **-(void)removeAllObjects** – Clear the array.

- **-(void)replaceObjectAtIndex:(NSUInteger)anIndex withObject:(id)anObject** – Overwrite the object at **anIndex** with **anObject**.

- `-(void)exchangeObjectAtIndex:(NSUInteger)index1 withObjectAtIndex:(NSUInteger)index2` – Swap the locations of two objects in the array.

Note that most of these mutable methods are essentially "write" methods, whereas the methods discussed in the NSArray section are mostly "read" methods. In addition, the mutable sort methods are the same as **NSArray**, except they sort the array *in place* instead of generating a new array. These differences are much the same as **NSString** versus **NSMutableString**. A simple example demonstrating the use of **NSMutableArray** as a queue follows:

```
// Define some people.
NSString *n1 = @"HAL";
NSString *n2 = @"Dave";
NSString *n3 = @"Heywood";

// Initialize an empty queue.
NSMutableArray *queue = [NSMutableArray arrayWithCapacity:4];

// Add to the queue.
[queue addObject:n1];
[queue addObject:n2];
[queue addObject:n3];

// Remove from the queue.
NSLog(@"Removing %@ from queue.", [queue objectAtIndex:0]);
[queue removeObjectAtIndex:0];
NSLog(@"Removing %@ from queue.", [queue objectAtIndex:0]);
[queue removeObjectAtIndex:0];
NSLog(@"Removing %@ from queue.", [queue objectAtIndex:0]);
[queue removeObjectAtIndex:0];
```

NSSet and NSMutableSet

Sets also represent a collection of objects, but unlike arrays, they are *unordered* collections. In addition, all of their elements must be unique. If you don't care about the order of elements or you want to make sure you don't have any duplicates in the collection, you should use NSSet and NSMutableSet instead of an array. In addition, sets are optimized for membership checking, so if your code is asking a lot of questions like, "Is this object in this group?" you should definitely be using a set instead of an array.

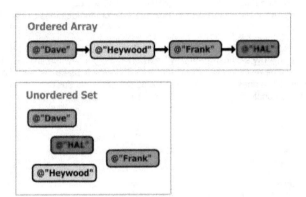

Figure 17: Ordered arrays vs. unordered sets

Data structures reflect the underlying relationships between their elements. The array interpretation of the previous figure could be something like, "Dave is in charge, then Heywood, then Frank, and finally HAL," whereas the set interpretation is more generic: "Dave, Heywood, Frank, and HAL are part of the crew."

Other than ordering, sets and arrays have very similar functions and APIs. Some of the most important methods are:

- `+(id)setWithObjects:(id)firstObject, ...` – Create a new set by passing a list of objects.
- `+(id)setWithArray:(NSArray)anArray` – Create a new set with the contents of an array. This is a simple way to remove duplicate items from an **NSArray**.
- `-(NSUInteger)count` – Return the number of members in the set.
- `-(BOOL)containsObject:(id)anObject` – Return **YES** if the specified object is a member of the set, **NO** otherwise. **NSArray** does have an identical method, but the **NSSet** version is more efficient.
- `-(NSArray *)allObjects` – Return an **NSArray** containing all of the set's members.

You can iterate through the members of a set using Objective-C's **fast-enumeration** syntax, as demonstrated in the following sample. Note that since **NSSet** is unordered, there is no guarantee as to how the objects will appear during the iteration:

```
NSSet *crew = [NSSet setWithObjects:@"Dave", @"Heywood", @"Frank", @"HAL", nil];
for (id member in crew) {
    NSLog(@"%@", member);
}
```

The Foundation framework also provides a mutable version of NSSet called NSMutableSet. Like NSMutableArray, you can alter a mutable set after creating it. Some of these "write" methods are:

- **-(void)addObject:(id)anObject** – Add the specified object to the set. Duplicate members will be ignored.

- **-(void)removeObject:(id)anObject** – Remove the specified object from the set.

- **-(void)unionSet:(NSSet *)otherSet** – Add each item in **otherSet** to the receiving set if it's not already a member.

Both the immutable and mutable versions of NSSet provide several other methods for logical operations like intersections and equality. Please see the official reference for more information.

NSDictionary and NSMutableDictionary

Dictionaries, also called associative arrays, are unordered associations of key-value pairs. It's possible to use any object as a key or a value, so dictionaries can be used for anything from dynamically assigning roles to objects to mapping string commands to functions.

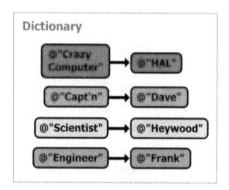

Figure 18: Unordered key-value pairs

Like strings, arrays, and sets, there is an immutable and a mutable version. Some of the most common methods for NSDictionary are:

- **+(id)dictionaryWithObjectsAndKeys:(id)firstValue, (id)firstKey, ...** – Create a dictionary by passing key-value pairs as parameters. Every two objects in the parameter list define a pair, and the first object defines the value, while the second object defines the key for that value (see next example for usage).

- **-(NSUInteger)count** – Return the number of entries in the dictionary.

- **-(id)objectForKey:(id)aKey** – Return the object (value) associated with **aKey**, or nil if there is no entry for **aKey**.

- **-(NSArray *)allKeys** – Return a new array containing all of the keys in the dictionary.

- -(NSArray *)allValues – Return a new array containing all of the values in the dictionary.
- -(NSArray *)allKeysForObject:(id)anObject – Return a new array containing all of the keys associated with **anObject**. Note that it's possible to have multiple keys associated with a single object, so keys must be returned as an array, not a single object.

The two core methods for **NSMutableDictionary** are described in the following list. Again, note that these are the "write" methods for the associated "read" methods of **NSDictionary**.

- -(void)setObject:(id)anObject forKey:(id<NSCopying>)aKey – Add a new key-value pair to the dictionary. The **aKey** argument must conform to the **NSCopying** protocol (refer to the Protocols chapter for more information). All of the objects we've discussed so far conform to this protocol, so you don't need to worry about it unless you're using custom classes as keys.
- -(void)removeObjectForKey:(id)aKey – Remove the entry using **aKey** as its key.

Like **NSSet**, dictionaries can be iterated over using the fast-enumeration syntax, as demonstrated here:

```
NSMutableDictionary *crew = [NSMutableDictionary
dictionaryWithObjectsAndKeys:@"Dave", @"Capt'n",
                             @"Heywood", @"Scientist",
                             @"Frank", @"Engineer", nil];

[crew setObject:@"HAL" forKey:@"Crazy Computer"];
[crew removeObjectForKey:@"Engineer"];

for (id role in crew) {
    NSLog(@"%@: %@", role, [crew objectForKey:role]);
}
```

This should output the following in your console, although the items may appear in a different order:

```
Scientist: Heywood
Crazy Computer: HAL
Capt'n: Dave
```

The id Data Type

While not technically a part of the Foundation framework, this is an appropriate time to introduce the **id** type, which is the generic object data type. It can hold a pointer to *any* Objective-C object, regardless of its class. This makes it possible to store different kinds of objects in a single variable, opening the door to dynamic programming. For example, **id** lets you store an **NSNumber**, an **NSDecimalNumber**, or an **NSString** in the same variable:

```
id mysteryObject = [NSNumber numberWithInt:5];
NSLog(@"%@", mysteryObject);

mysteryObject = [NSDecimalNumber decimalNumberWithString:@"5.1"];
NSLog(@"%@", mysteryObject);

mysteryObject = @"5.2";
NSLog(@"%@", mysteryObject);
```

Note that **id** implies that the value will be a pointer, so variable declarations don't require an asterisk before the variable name. In other words, variables should always be declared as **id mysteryObject**, not **id *mysteryObject**.

Since an **id** variable doesn't check what kind of object it contains, it's the *programmer's* responsibility to makes sure he or she doesn't call methods or access properties that aren't defined on the object (e.g., don't try to call **stringValue** when the variable contains an **NSString** instance.

The Class Data Type

Objective-C classes are actually objects themselves, and they can be stored in variables using the **Class** type. You can get the class object associated with a particular class by sending it the **class** message. The following example shows how to retrieve a class object, store it in a **Class** variable, and use it to figure out which kind of object is stored in an **id** variable:

```
Class targetClass = [NSString class];

id mysteryObject = [NSNumber numberWithInt:5];
NSLog(@"%i", [mysteryObject isKindOfClass:targetClass]);

mysteryObject = [NSDecimalNumber decimalNumberWithString:@"5.1"];
NSLog(@"%i", [mysteryObject isKindOfClass:targetClass]);

mysteryObject = @"5.2";
NSLog(@"%i", [mysteryObject isKindOfClass:targetClass]);
```

The **Class** data type brings the same dynamic capabilities to classes that **id** brings to objects.

Foundation Data Structures Summary

The classes presented in the latter half of this chapter provide the foundation to nearly every Objective-C program. Strings, arrays, sets, and dictionaries are the core of nearly every programming language, and having such a high-level interface for representing data is an important aspect of productivity. We also saw how Objective-C needs to box C primitives for use with these Foundation framework classes, which provides a convenient API at the expense of performance and memory. Of course, you're always free to work with primitive data types in an Objective-C program.

We also examined two more object-oriented data types available to Objective-C applications: **id** and **Class**. Together, these open up a wide variety of possibilities for organizing an application.

Chapter 3 Properties

Now that we've explored what data types are available, we can talk about actually using them in a productive manner. We learned how to declare properties in Hello, Objective-C, but this chapter dives deeper into the nuances behind public properties and instance variables. First, we'll take a quick look at the basic syntax of properties and instance variables, and then we'll discuss how to use behavior attributes to modify accessor methods.

Declaring Properties

Properties can be declared in an interface using the **@property** directive. As a quick review, let's take a look at the **Person.h** file we created in the Hello, Objective-C chapter:

```
#import <Foundation/Foundation.h>

@interface Person : NSObject

@property (copy) NSString *name;

@end
```

This declares a property called **name** of type **NSString**. The **(copy)** attribute tells the runtime what to do when someone tries to set the value of **name**. In this case, it creates an independent copy of the value instead of pointing to the existing object. We'll talk more about this in the next chapter, Memory Management.

Implementing Properties

In Hello, Objective-C, we used the **@synthesize** directive to automatically create getter and setter methods. Remember that the getter method is simply the name of the property, and the default setter method is **setName**:

```
#import "Person.h"

@implementation Person

@synthesize name = _name;

@end
```

But, it's also possible to manually create the accessor methods. Doing this manually helps to understand what **@property** and **@synthesize** are doing behind the scenes.

Included code sample: ManualProperty

First, add a new property to the **Person** interface:

```
@property (copy) NSString *name;
@property unsigned int age;
```

Note that we're storing **age** as a primitive data type (not a pointer to an object), so it doesn't need an asterisk before the property name. Back in **Person.m**, define the accessor methods explicitly:

```
- (unsigned int)age {
    return _age;
}

- (void)setAge:(unsigned int)age {
    _age = age;
}
```

This is exactly what **@synthesize** would have done for us, but now we have the chance to validate values before they are assigned. We are, however, missing one thing: the **_age** instance variable. **@synthesize** automatically created a **_name** ivar, allowing us to forgo this for the **name** property.

Instance Variables

Instance variables, also known as ivars, are variables intended to be used inside of the class. They can be declared inside of curly braces after either the **@interface** or **@implementation** directives. For example, in **Person.h**, change the interface declaration to the following:

```
@interface Person {
    unsigned int _age;
}
```

This defines an instance variable called **_age**, so this class should now compile successfully. By default, instance variables declared in an interface are *protected.* The equivalent C# class definition would be something like:

```
class Person {
    protected uint _age;
}
```

Objective-C scope modifiers are the same as in C#: private variables are only accessible to the containing class, protected variables are accessible to all subclasses, and public variables are available to other objects. You can define the scope of instance variables with the **@private**,

@protected, and **@public** directives inside of **@interface**, as demonstrated in the following code:

```
@interface Person : NSObject {
  @private
    NSString *_ssn;
  @protected
    unsigned int _age;
  @public
    NSString *job;
}
```

Public ivars are actually a bit outside Objective-C norms. A class with public variables acts more like a C struct than a class; instead of the usual messaging syntax, you need to use the -> pointer operator. For example:

```
Person *frank = [[Person alloc] init];
frank->job = @"Astronaut";
NSLog(@"%@", frank->job);
// NOT: [frank job];
```

However, in most cases, you'll want to hide implementation details by using an **@property** declaration instead of public instance variables. Furthermore, because instance variables are technically implementation details, many programmers like to keep *all* instance variables private. With this in mind, ivars declared in **@implementation** are private by default. So, if you were to move the **_age** declaration to **Person.m** instead of the header:

```
@implementation Person {
    unsigned int _age;
}
```

_age would be scoped as a *private* variable. Keep this in mind when working with instance variables in subclasses, as the different defaults for interface versus implementation declaration can be confusing for newcomers to Objective-C.

Customizing Accessors

But enough about instance variables; let's get back to properties. Accessor methods can be customized using several property declaration attributes (e.g., **(copy)**). Some of the most important attributes are:

- **getter=getterName** – Customize the name of the getter accessor method. Remember that the default is simply the name of the property.

- **setter=setterName** – Customize the name of the setter accessor method. Remember that the default is **set** followed by the name of the property (e.g., **setName**).

- **readonly** – Make the property read-only, meaning only a getter will be synthesized. By default, properties are read-write. This cannot be used with the **setter** attribute.

- **nonatomic** – Indicate that the accessor methods do not need to be thread safe. Properties are atomic by default, which means that Objective-C will use a lock/retain (described in the next chapter) to return the *complete* value from a getter/setter. Note, however, that this does *not* guarantee data integrity across threads—merely that getters and setters will be atomic. If you're not in a threaded environment, non-atomic properties are much faster.

A common use case for customizing getter names is for Boolean naming conventions. Many programmers like to prepend **is** to Boolean variable names. This is easy to implement via the **getter** attribute:

```
@property (getter=isEmployed) BOOL employed;
```

Internally, the class can use the **employed** variable, but other objects can use the **isEmployed** and **setEmployed** accessors to interact with the object:

```
Person *frank = [[Person alloc] init];
[frank setName:@"Frank"];
[frank setEmployed:YES];
if ([frank isEmployed]) {
    NSLog(@"Frank is employed");
} else {
    NSLog(@"Frank is unemployed");
}
```

Many of the other property attributes relate to memory management, which will be discussed in the upcoming section. It's also possible to apply multiple attributes to a single property by separating them with commas:

```
@property (getter=isEmployed, readonly) BOOL employed;
```

Dot Syntax

In addition to getter/setter methods, it's also possible to use dot notation to access declared properties. For C# developers, this should be much more familiar than Objective-C's square-bracket messaging syntax:

```
Person *frank = [[Person alloc] init];
frank.name = @"Frank";      // Same as [frank setName:@"Frank"];
NSLog(@"%@", frank.name); // Same as [frank name];
```

Note this is just a convenience—it translates directly to the getter/setter methods described previously. Dot notation *cannot* be used for instance methods.

Summary

Properties are an integral aspect of any object-oriented programming language. They are the data that methods operate on. The **@property** directive is a convenient way to configure a property's behavior, but it doesn't do anything that can't be done by manually creating getter and setter methods.

In the next chapter, we'll take a detailed look at how properties are stored in memory, as well as a few new property attributes for controlling this behavior. After that, we'll dive into methods, which rounds out the core object-oriented tools of Objective-C.

Chapter 4 Memory Management

Memory must be allocated for each object your application uses, and it must be deallocated when your application is done with it to ensure your application is using memory as efficiently as possible. It's important to understand Objective-C's memory management environment to ensure your program doesn't leak memory or try to reference objects that no longer exist.

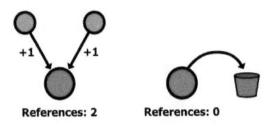

Figure 19: Counting references to an object

Unlike C#, Objective-C does *not* use garbage collection. Instead, it uses a reference-counting environment that tracks how many places are using an object. As long as there is at least one reference to the object, the Objective-C runtime makes sure the object will reside in memory. However, if there are no longer any references to the object, the runtime is allowed to release the object and use the memory for something else. If you try to access an object after it has been released, your program will most likely crash.

There are two mutually exclusive ways to manage object references in Objective-C:

1. Manually send methods to increment/decrement the number of references to an object.

2. Let Xcode 4.2's (and later) new automatic reference counting (ARC) scheme do the work for you.

ARC is the preferred way to manage memory in new applications, but it's still important to understand what's going on under the hood. The first part of this chapter shows you how to manually track object references, and then we'll talk about the practical implications of ARC.

Manual Memory Management

To experiment with any of the code in this section, you'll need to turn off automatic reference counting. You can do this by clicking the **HelloObjectiveC** project in Xcode's navigation panel:

Figure 20: The HelloObjectiveC project in the navigation panel

This opens a window to let you adjust the build settings for the project. We'll discuss build settings in the second half of this series. For now, all we need to find is the ARC flag. In the search field in the upper-right corner, type **automatic reference counting**, and you should see the following setting appear:

Figure 21: Disabling automatic reference counting

Click the arrows next to **Yes** and change it to **No** to disable ARC for this project. This will let you use the memory management methods discussed in the following paragraphs.

Manual memory management (also called manual retain-release or MMR) revolves around the concept of object "ownership." When you create an object, you're said to *own* the object—it's your responsibility to free the object when you're done with it. This makes sense, since you wouldn't want some other object to come along and release the object while you're using it.

Object ownership is implemented through reference counting. When you claim ownership of an object, you increase its reference count by one, and when you relinquish ownership, you decrement its reference count by one. In this way, it's possible to ensure that an object will never be freed from memory while another object is using it. NSObject and the NSObject protocol define the four core methods that support object ownership:

- **+(id)alloc** – Allocate memory for a new instance and claim ownership of that instance. This increases the object's reference count by one. It returns a pointer to the allocated object.

- **-(id)retain** – Claim ownership of an existing object. It's possible for an object to have more than one owner. This also increments the object's reference count. It returns a pointer to the existing object.

- **-(void)release** – Relinquish ownership of an object. This decrements the object's reference count.

- **-(id)autorelease** – Relinquish ownership of an object at the end of the current autorelease pool block. This decrements the object's reference count, but lets you keep using the object by deferring the actual release until a later point in time. It returns a pointer to the existing object.

For every **alloc** or **retain** method you call, you need to call **release** or **autorelease** at some point down the line. The number of times you claim an object *must* equal the number of times you release it. Calling an extra **alloc/retain** will result in a memory leak, and calling an extra **release/autorelease** will try to access an object that doesn't exist, causing your program to crash.

All of your object interactions—regardless of whether you're using them in an instance method, getter/setter, or a stand-alone function—should follow the claim/use/free pattern, as demonstrated in the following sample:

Included code sample: Manual Memory

```
int main(int argc, const char * argv[]) {

    // Claim the object.
    Person *frank = [[Person alloc] init];

    // Use the object.
    frank.name = @"Frank";
    NSLog(@"%@", frank.name);

    // Free the object.
    [frank release];

    return 0;
}
```

The [Person alloc] call sets frank's reference count to one, and [frank release] decrements it to zero, allowing the runtime to dispose of it. Note that trying to call another [frank release] would result in a crash, since the frank variable no longer exists in memory.

When using objects as a local variable in a function (e.g., the previous example), memory management is pretty straightforward: simply call **release** at the end of the function. However, things can get trickier when assigning properties inside of setter methods. For example, consider the following interface for a new class called **Ship**:

Included code sample: Manual Memory – weak reference

```
// Ship.h
#import "Person.h"

@interface Ship : NSObject

- (Person *)captain;
- (void)setCaptain:(Person *)theCaptain;

@end
```

This is a very simple class with manually defined accessor methods for a **captain** property. From a memory-management perspective, there are several ways the setter can be implemented. First, take the simplest case where the new value is simply assigned to an instance variable:

```
// Ship.m
#import "Ship.h"

@implementation Ship {
    Person *_captain;
}
```

```
- (Person *)captain {
    return _captain;
}

- (void)setCaptain:(Person *)theCaptain {
    _captain = theCaptain;
}

@end
```

This creates a *weak reference* because the **Ship** instance doesn't take ownership of the **theCaptain** object when it gets assigned. While there's nothing wrong with this, and your code will still work, it's important to understand the implications of weak references. Consider the following snippet:

```
#import <Foundation/Foundation.h>
#import "Person.h"
#import "Ship.h"

int main(int argc, const char * argv[]) {
    @autoreleasepool {

        Person *frank = [[Person alloc] init];
        Ship *discoveryOne = [[Ship alloc] init];

        frank.name = @"Frank";
        [discoveryOne setCaptain:frank];
        NSLog(@"%@", [discoveryOne captain].name);

        [frank release];

        // [discoveryOne captain] is now invalid.
        NSLog(@"%@", [discoveryOne captain]. name);

        [discoveryOne release];
    }
    return 0;
}
```

Calling [**frank release**] decrements **frank**'s reference count to zero, which means the runtime is allowed to deallocate it. This means that [**discoveryOne captain**] now points to an invalid memory address, even though **discoveryOne** never released it.

In the sample code provided, you will observe that we have added a **dealloc** method override in the Person class. **dealloc** is called when memory is about to be released. We should typically handle **dealloc** and release any nested object references that we hold. In this instance we will release the nested name property that we hold. We will have more to say about **dealloc** in the next chapter.

If you were to try to access the property, your program would most likely crash. As you can see, you need to be very careful tracking object references when you use weakly referenced properties.

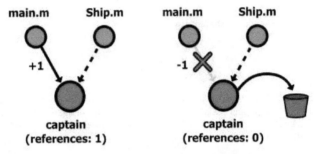

Figure 22: Weak reference to the `captain` value

For more robust object relationships, you can use strong references. These are created by claiming the object with a **retain** call when it is assigned:

Included code sample: Manual Memory - strong reference

```
- (void)setCaptain:(Person *)theCaptain {
    [_captain autorelease];
    _captain = [theCaptain retain];
}
```

With a strong reference, it doesn't matter what other objects are doing with the **theCaptain** object, since **retain** makes sure it will stay around as long as the **Ship** instance needs it. Of course, you need to balance the **retain** call by releasing the old value—if you didn't, your program would leak memory whenever anyone assigned a new value to the **captain** property.

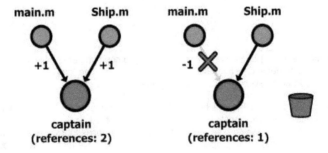

Figure 23: Strong reference to the `captain` *value*

Auto-Releasing Objects

The `autorelease` method works much like `release`, except the object's reference count isn't decremented immediately. Instead, the runtime waits until the end of the current `@autoreleasepool` block to call a normal `release` on the object. This is why the `main.m` template is always wrapped in an `@autoreleasepool`—it makes sure all objects queued with `autorelease` calls are *actually* released at the end of the program:

```
int main(int argc, const char * argv[]) {

    @autoreleasepool {

        // Insert code to create and autorelease objects here.
        NSLog(@"Hello, World!");

        // Any autoreleased objects are *actually* released here.
    }
    return 0;
}
```

The idea behind auto-releasing is to give an object's owner the ability to relinquish ownership without actually destroying the object. This is a necessary tool in situations where you need to return a new object from a factory method. For example, consider the following class method defined in `Ship.m`:

```
+ (Ship *)shipWithCaptain:(Person *)theCaptian {
    Ship *theShip = [[Ship alloc] init];
    [theShip setCaptain:theCaptian];
    return theShip;
}
```

This method creates, configures, and returns a new `Ship` instance. But there's a serious problem with this implementation: it results in a memory leak. The method never relinquishes ownership of the object, and callers of `shipWithCaptain` don't know that they need to free the returned object (nor should they have to). As a result, the `theShip` object will never be released from memory. This is precisely the situation `autorelease` was designed for. The proper implementation is shown here:

```
+ (Ship *)shipWithCaptain:(Person *)theCaptian {
    Ship *theShip = [[Ship alloc] init];
    [theShip setCaptain:theCaptian];
    return [theShip autorelease];        // Must relinquish ownership!
}
```

Using `autorelease` instead of an immediate `release` lets the caller use the returned object while still relinquishing ownership of it in the proper location. If you remember from the Data

<u>Types</u> chapter, we created all of our Foundation data structures using class-level factory methods. For example:

```
NSSet *crew = [NSSet setWithObjects:@"Dave", @"Heywood", @"Frank", @"HAL", nil];
```

The **setWithObjects** method works exactly like the **shipWithCaptain** method described in the previous example. It returns an autoreleased object so that the caller can use the object without worrying about memory management. Note that there are equivalent instance methods for initializing Foundation objects. For example, the **crew** object in the last sample can be manually created as follows:

```
// Create and claim the set.
NSSet *crew = [[NSSet alloc] initWithObjects:@"Dave", @"Heywood", @"Frank", @"HAL",
nil];

// Use the set...

// Release the set.
[crew release];
```

However, using class methods like **setWithObjects**, **arrayWithCapacity**, etc., is generally preferred over the **alloc/init**.

Manual Retain-Release Attributes

Dealing with the memory behind an object's properties can be a tedious, repetitive task. To simplify the process, Objective-C includes several property attributes for automating the memory management calls in accessor functions. The attributes described in the following list define the setter behavior in *manual* reference-counting environments. Do *not* try to use **assign** and **retain** in an automatic reference counting environment.

- **assign** – Store a direct pointer to the new value without any **retain/release** calls. This is the automated equivalent of a weak reference.
- **retain** – Store a direct pointer to the new value, but call **release** on the old value and **retain** on the new one. This is the automated equivalent of a strong reference.
- **copy** – Create a copy of the new value. Copying claims ownership of the new instance, so the previous value is sent a **release** message. This is like a strong reference to a brand new instance of the object. Generally, copying is only used for immutable types like **NSString**.

As a simple example, examine the following property declaration:

```
@property (retain) Person *captain;
```

The **retain** attribute tells the associated **@synthesize** declaration to create a setter that looks something like:

```
- (void)setCaptain:(Person *)theCaptain {
    [_captain release];
    _captain = [theCaptain retain];
}
```

As you can imagine, using memory management attributes with **@property** is much easier than manually defining getters and setters for every property of every custom class you define.

Automatic Reference Counting

Now that you've got a handle on reference counting, object ownership, and autorelease blocks, you can completely forget about all of it. As of Xcode 4.2 and iOS 4, Objective-C supports automatic reference counting (ARC), which is a pre-compilation step that adds in the necessary memory management calls for you.

If you happened to have turned off ARC in the previous section, you should turn it back on. Remember that you can do this by clicking on the **HelloObjectiveC** project in the navigation panel, selecting the **Build Settings** tab, and searching for **automatic reference counting**.

Figure 24: Enabling Automatic Reference Counting in the project's build settings

Automatic reference counting works by examining your code to figure out how long an object needs to stick around and inserting **retain**, **release**, and **autorelease** methods to ensure it's deallocated when no longer needed, but not while you're using it. So as not to confuse the ARC algorithm, you *must not* make any **retain**, **release**, or **autorelease** calls yourself. For example, with ARC, you can write the following method and neither **theShip** nor **theCaptain** will be leaked, even though we didn't explicitly relinquish ownership of them:

Included code sample: ARC

```
+ (Ship *)ship {
    Ship *theShip = [[Ship alloc] init];
    Person *theCaptain = [[Person alloc] init];
    [theShip setCaptain:theCaptain];
    return theShip;
}
```

ARC Attributes

In an ARC environment, you should no longer use the **assign** and **retain** property attributes. Instead, you should use the **weak** and **strong** attributes:

- **weak** – Specify a non-owning relationship to the destination object. This is much like **assign**; however, it has the convenient functionality of setting the property to **nil** if the value is deallocated. This way, your program won't crash when it tries to access an invalid memory address.

- **strong** – Specify an owning relationship to the destination object. This is the ARC equivalent of **retain**. It ensures that an object won't be released as long as it's assigned to the property.

You can see the difference between weak and strong using the implementation of the **ship** class method from the previous section. To create a strong reference to the ship's captain, the interface for **Ship** should look like the following:

```
// Ship.h
#import "Person.h"

@interface Ship : NSObject

@property (strong) Person *captain;

+ (Ship *)ship;

@end
```

And the implementation **Ship** should look like:

```
// Ship.m
#import "Ship.h"

@implementation Ship

@synthesize captain = _captain;

+ (Ship *)ship {
    Ship *theShip = [[Ship alloc] init];
    Person *theCaptain = [[Person alloc] init];
    [theShip setCaptain:theCaptain];
    return theShip;
}

@end
```

Then, you can change **main.m** to display the ship's captain:

```
int main(int argc, const char * argv[]) {
    @autoreleasepool {
        Ship *ship = [Ship ship];
        NSLog(@"%@", [ship captain]);
    }
    return 0;
}
```

This will output something like **<Person: 0x7fd6c8c14560>** in the console, which tells us that the **theCaptain** object created in the **ship** class method still exists.

But, try changing the **(strong)** property attribute to **(weak)** and re-compiling the program. Now, you should see **(null)** in the output panel. The weak reference doesn't ensure that the **theCaptain** variable sticks around, so once it arrives at the end of the **ship** class method, the ARC algorithm thinks that it can dispose of **theCaptain**. As a result, the **captain** property is set to **nil**.

Summary

Memory management can be a pain, but it's an essential part of building an application. For iOS applications, proper object allocation/disposal is particularly important because of the limited memory resources of mobile devices. We'll talk more about this in the second part of this series, *iOS Succinctly*.

Fortunately, the new ARC scheme makes memory management much easier on the average developer. In most cases, it's possible to treat an ARC project just like the garbage collection in a C# program—just create your objects and let ARC dispose of them at its discretion. Note, however, that this is merely a practical similarity—the ARC implementation is much more efficient than garbage collection.

Chapter 5 Methods

In this chapter, we'll explore Objective-C methods in much more detail than we have in previous chapters. This includes an in-depth discussion of instance methods, class methods, important built-in methods, inheritance, naming conventions, and common design patterns.

Instance vs. Class Methods

We've been working with both instance and class methods throughout this book, but let's take a moment to formalize the two major categories of methods in Objective-C:

- **Instance methods** – Functions bound to an object. Instance methods are the "verbs" associated with an object.

- **Class methods** – Functions bound to the class itself. They cannot be used by instances of the class. These are similar to static methods in C#.

As we've seen many times, instance methods are denoted by a hyphen before the method name, whereas class methods are prefixed with a plus sign. For example, let's take a simplified version of our **Person.h** file:

```
@interface Person : NSObject

@property (copy) NSString *name;

- (void)sayHello;
+ (Person *)personWithName:(NSString *)name;

@end
```

Likewise, the corresponding implementation methods also need to be preceded by a hyphen or a plus sign. So, a minimal **Person.m** might look something like:

```
#import "Person.h"

@implementation Person

@synthesize name = _name;

- (void)sayHello {
    NSLog(@"HELLO");
}

+ (Person *)personWithName:(NSString *)name {
    Person *person = [[Person alloc] init];
    person.name = name;
```

```
    return person;
}

@end
```

The **sayHello** method can be called by *instances* of the **Person** class, whereas the **personWithName** method can only be called by the class itself:

```
Person *p1 = [Person personWithName:@"Frank"];   // Class method.
[p1 sayHello];                                     // Instance method.
```

Most of this should be familiar to you by now, but now we have the opportunity to talk about some of the unique conventions in Objective-C.

The super Keyword

In any object-oriented environment, it's important to be able to access methods from the parent class. Objective-C uses a very similar scheme to C#, except instead of **base**, it uses the **super** keyword. For example, the following implementation of **sayHello** would display **HELLO** in the output panel, and then call the parent class' version of **sayHello**:

```
- (void)sayHello {
    NSLog(@"HELLO");
    [super sayHello];
}
```

Unlike in C#, override methods do not need to be explicitly marked as such. You'll see this with both the **init** and **dealloc** methods discussed in the following section. Even though these are defined on the **NSObject** class, the compiler doesn't complain when you create your own **init** and **dealloc** methods in subclasses.

Initialization Methods

Initialization methods are required for all objects—a newly allocated object is not considered "ready to use" until one of its initialization methods has been called. They are the place to set defaults for instance variables and otherwise set up the state of the object. The **NSObject** class defines a default **init** method that doesn't do anything, but it's often useful to create your own. For example, a custom **init** implementation for our **Ship** class could assign default values to an instance variable called **_ammo**:

```
- (id)init {
    self = [super init];
    if (self) {
        _ammo = 1000;
```

```
    }
    return self;
}
```

This is the canonical way to define a custom **init** method. The **self** keyword is the equivalent of C#'s **this**—it's used to refer to the instance calling the method, which makes it possible for an object to send messages to itself. As you can see, all **init** methods are required to return the instance. This is what makes it possible to use the [[**Ship alloc**] **init**] syntax to assign the instance to a variable. Also notice that because the **NSObject** interface declares the **init** method, there is no need to add an **init** declaration to **Ship.h**.

While simple **init** methods like the one shown in the previous sample are useful for setting default instance variable values, it's often more convenient to pass parameters to an initialization method:

```
- (id)initWithAmmo:(unsigned int)theAmmo {
    self = [super init];
    if (self) {
        _ammo = theAmmo;
    }
    return self;
}
```

A Brief Aside on Method Names

If you're coming from a C# background, you might be uncomfortable with the **initWithAmmo** method name. You'd probably expect to see the **Ammo** parameter separated from the actual method name like **void init(uint ammo)**; however, Objective-C method naming is based on an entirely different philosophy.

Recall that Objective-C's goal is to force an API to be as descriptive as possible, ensuring that there is absolutely no confusion as to what a method call is going to do. You can't think of a method as a separate entity from its parameters—they are a single unit. This design decision is actually reflected in Objective-C's implementation, which makes no distinction between a method and its parameters. Internally, a method name is actually the *concatenated parameter list*.

For example, consider the following three method declarations. Note that the second and third are not built-in methods of **NSObject**, so you *do* need to add them to the class' interface before implementing them.

```
- (id)init;
- (id)initWithAmmo:(unsigned int)theAmmo;
- (id)initWithAmmo:(unsigned int)theAmmo captain:(Person *)theCaptain;
```

While this looks like method overloading, it's technically not. These are not variations on the `init` method—they are all completely independent methods with distinct method names. The names of these methods are as follows:

```
init
initWithAmmo:
initWithAmmo:captain:
```

This is the reason you see notation like **indexOfObjectWithOptions:passingTest:** and **indexOfObjectAtIndexes:options:passingTest:** for referring to methods in the official Objective-C documentation (taken from NSArray).

From a practical standpoint, this means that the first parameter of your methods should always be described by the "primary" method name. Ambiguous methods like the following are generally frowned upon by Objective-C programmers:

```
- (id)shoot:(Ship *)aShip;
```

Instead, you should use a preposition to include the first parameter in the method name, like so:

```
- (id)shootOtherShip:(Ship *)aShip;
```

Including both **OtherShip** and **aShip** in the method definition may seem redundant, but remember that the **aShip** argument is only used internally. Someone calling the method is going to write something like **shootOtherShip:discoveryOne**, where **discoveryOne** is the variable containing the ship you want to shoot. This is exactly the kind of verbosity that Objective-C developers strive for.

Class Initialization

In addition to the `init` method for initializing *instances*, Objective-C also provides a way to set up *classes*. Before calling any class methods or instantiating any objects, the Objective-C runtime calls the `initialize` class method of the class in question. This gives you the opportunity to define any static variables before anyone uses the class. One of the most common use cases for this is to set up singletons:

```
static Ship *_sharedShip;

+ (void)initialize {
    if (self == [Ship class]) {
        _sharedShip = [[self alloc] init];
    }
}

+ (Ship *)sharedShip {
    return _sharedShip;
```

```
}
```

Before the first time [Ship sharedShip] is called, the runtime will call [Ship initialize], which makes sure the singleton is defined. The static variable modifier serves the same purpose as it does in C#—it creates a class-level variable instead of an instance variable. The initialize method is only called once, but it's called on all super classes, so you have to take care not to initialize class-level variables multiple times. This is why we included the self == [Ship class] conditional to make sure _shareShip is only allocated in the Ship class.

Also note that inside of a class method, the self keyword refers to the class itself, not an instance. So, [self alloc] in the last example is the equivalent of [Ship alloc].

Deallocation Methods

The logical counterpart to an instance's initialization method is the dealloc method. This method is called on an object when its reference count reaches zero and its underlying memory is about to be deallocated.

Deallocation in MMR

If you're using manual memory management (not recommended), you need to release any instance variables that your object allocated in the dealloc method. If you don't free instance variables before your object goes out of scope, you'll have dangling pointers to your instance variables, which means leaked memory whenever an instance of the class is released. For example, if our Ship class allocated a variable called _gun in its init method, you would have to release it in dealloc. This is demonstrated in the following example (Gun.h contains an empty interface that simply defines the Gun class):

```
#import "Ship.h"
#import "Gun.h"


@implementation Ship {
    BOOL _gunIsReady;
    Gun *_gun;
}

- (id)init {
    self = [super init];
    if (self) {
        _gun = [[Gun alloc] init];
    }
    return self;
}

- (void)dealloc {
    NSLog(@"Deallocating a Ship");
    [_gun release];
```

```
        [super dealloc];
}

@end
```

You can see the **dealloc** method in action by creating a **Ship** and releasing it, like so:

```
int main(int argc, const char * argv[]) {
    @autoreleasepool {
        Ship *ship = [[Ship alloc] init];
        [ship autorelease];
        NSLog(@"Ship should still exist in autoreleasepool");
    }
    NSLog(@"Ship should be deallocated by now");
    return 0;
}
```

This also demonstrates how auto-released objects work. The **dealloc** method won't be called until the end of the **@autoreleasepool** block, so the previous code should output the following:

```
Ship should still exist in autoreleasepool
Deallocating a Ship
Ship should be deallocated by now
```

Note that the first **NSLog()** message in **main()** is displayed *before* the one in the **dealloc** method, even though it was called *after* the **autorelease** call.

Deallocation in ARC

However, if you're using automatic reference counting, all of your instance variables will be deallocated automatically, and [**super dealloc**] will be called for you as well (you should never call it explicitly). So, the only thing you have to worry about are non-object variables like buffers created with C's **malloc()**.

Like **init**, you don't have to implement a **dealloc** method if your object doesn't need any special handling before it is released. This is often the case for automatic reference-counting environments.

Private Methods

A big hurdle for C# developers transitioning to Objective-C is the apparent lack of private methods. Unlike C#, all methods in an Objective-C class are accessible to third parties; however, it is possible to *emulate* the behavior of private methods.

Remember that clients only import the interface of a class (i.e. the header files)—they should never see the underlying implementation. So, by adding new methods inside of the *implementation* file without including them in the *interface*, we can effectively hide methods from other objects. Albeit, this is more convention-based than "true" private methods, but it's essentially the same functionality: trying to call a method that's not declared in an interface will result in a compiler error.

Figure 25: Attempting to call a "private" method

For example, let's say you needed to add a private **prepareToShoot** method to the **Ship** class. All you have to do is omit it from **Ship.h** while adding it to **Ship.m**:

```
// Ship.h
@interface Ship : NSObject

@property (weak) Person *captain;

- (void)shoot;

@end
```

This declares a public method called **shoot**, which will use the private **prepareToShoot** method. The corresponding implementation might look something like:

```
// Ship.m
#import "Ship.h"

@implementation Ship {
    BOOL _gunIsReady;
}

@synthesize captain = _captain;

- (void)shoot {
    if (!_gunIsReady) {
        [self prepareToShoot];
        _gunIsReady = YES;
    }
    NSLog(@"Firing!");
}

- (void)prepareToShoot {
    // Execute some private functionality.
    NSLog(@"Preparing the main weapon...");
}

@end
```

As of Xcode 4.3, you can define private methods *anywhere* in the implementation. If you use the private method before the compiler has seen it (as in the previous example), the compiler checks the rest of the implementation block for the method definition. Prior to Xcode 4.3, you had to either define a private method *before* it was used elsewhere in the file, or forward-declare it with a **class extension**.

Class extensions are a special case of **categories**, which are presented in the upcoming chapter. Just as there is no way to mark a method as private, there is no way to mark a method as protected; however, as we'll see in the next chapter, categories provide a powerful alternative to protected methods.

Selectors

Selectors are Objective-C's way of representing methods. They let you dynamically "select" one of an object's methods, which can be used to refer to a method at run time, pass a method to another function, and figure out whether an object has a particular method. For practical purposes, you can think of a selector as an alternative name for a method.

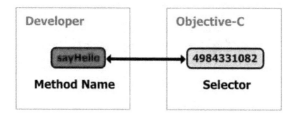

Figure 26: Developers' representation of a method vs. Objective-C's representation

Internally, Objective-C uses a unique number to identify each method name that your program uses. For instance, a method called **sayHello** might translate to **4984331082**. This identifier is called a **selector**, and it is a much more efficient way for the compiler to refer to methods than their full string representation. It's important to understand that a selector only represents the method *name*—not a specific method implementation. In other words, a **sayHello** method defined by the **Person** class has the same selector as a **sayHello** method defined by the **Ship** class.

The three main tools for working with selectors are:

- **@selector()** – Return the selector associated with a source-code method name.
- **NSSelectorFromString()** – Return the selector associated with the string representation of a method name. This function makes it possible to define the method name at run time, but it is less efficient than **@selector()**.
- **NSStringFromSelector()** – Return the string representation of a method name from a selector.

As you can see, there are three ways to represent a method name in Objective-C: as source code, as a string, or as a selector. These conversion functions are shown graphically in the following figure:

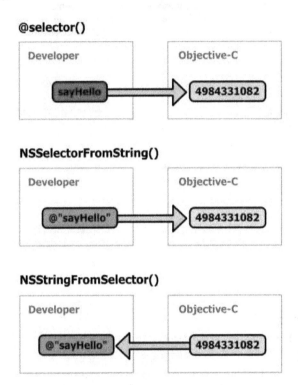

Figure 27: Converting between source code, strings, and selectors

Selectors are stored in a special data type called **SEL**. The following snippet demonstrates the basic usage of the three conversion functions shown in the previous figure:

```
int main(int argc, const char * argv[]) {
    @autoreleasepool {

        SEL selector = @selector(sayHello);
        NSLog(@"%@", NSStringFromSelector(selector));
        if (selector == NSSelectorFromString(@"sayHello")) {
            NSLog(@"The selectors are equal!");
        }

    }
}
```

```
        return 0;
}
```

First, we use the **@selector()** directive to figure out the selector for a method called **sayHello**, which is a source-code representation of a method name. Note that you can pass *any* method name to **@selector()**—it doesn't have to exist elsewhere in your program. Next, we use the **NSStringFromSelector()** function to convert the selector back into a string so we can display it in the output panel. Finally, the conditional shows that selectors have a one-to-one correspondence with method names, regardless of whether you find them through hard-coded method names or strings.

Method Names and Selectors

The previous example uses a simple method that takes no parameters, but it's important to be able to pass around methods that *do* accept parameters. Recall that a method name consists of the primary method name concatenated with all of the parameter names. For example, a method with the *signature*

```
- (void)sayHelloToPerson:(Person *)aPerson
            withGreeting:(NSString *)aGreeting;
```

would have a method *name* of:

```
sayHelloToPerson:withGreeting:
```

This is what you would pass to **@selector()** or **NSSelectorFromString()** to return the identifier for that method. Selectors only work with method *names* (not signatures), so there is *not* a one-to-one correspondence between selectors and signatures. As a result, the method *name* in the last example will also match a signature with different data types, including the following:

```
- (void)sayHelloToPerson:(NSString *)aName
            withGreeting:(BOOL)useGreeting;
```

The verbosity of Objective-C's naming conventions avoids most confusing situations; however, selectors for one-parameter methods can still be tricky because appending a colon to the method name actually changes it into a *completely different* method. For example, in the following sample, the first method name doesn't take a parameter, while the second one does:

```
sayHello
sayHello:
```

Again, naming conventions go a long way toward eliminating confusion, but you still need to make sure you know when it's necessary to add a colon to the end of a method name. This is a common issue if you're new to selectors, and it can be hard to debug, as a trailing colon still creates a perfectly valid method name.

Performing Selectors

Of course, recording a selector in a **SEL** variable is relatively useless without the ability to execute it later on. Since a selector is merely a method *name* (not an implementation), it always needs to be paired with an object before you can call it. The **NSObject** class defines a **performSelector:** method for this very purpose.

```
[joe performSelector:@selector(sayHello)];
```

This is the equivalent of calling **sayHello** directly on **joe**:

```
[joe sayHello];
```

For methods with one or two parameters, you can use the related **performSelector:withObject:** and **performSelector:withObject:withObject:** methods. The following method implementation:

```
- (void)sayHelloToPerson:(Person *)aPerson {
    NSLog(@"Hello, %@", [aPerson name]);
}
```

could be called dynamically by passing the **aPerson** argument to the **performSelector:withObject:** method, as demonstrated here:

```
[joe performSelector:@selector(sayHelloToPerson:) withObject:bill];
```

This is the equivalent of passing the parameter directly to the method:

```
[joe sayHelloToPerson:bill];
```

Likewise, the **performSelector:withObject:withObject:** method lets you pass two parameters to the target method. The only caveat with these is that all parameters and the return value of the method must be objects—they don't work with primitive C data types like **int**, **float**, etc. If you do need this functionality, you can either box the primitive type in one of Objective-C's many wrapper classes (e.g., **NSNumber**) or use the NSInvocation object to encapsulate a complete method call.

Checking for the Existence of Selectors

It's not possible to perform a selector on an object that hasn't defined the associated method. But unlike static method calls, it's not possible to determine at compile time whether

performSelector: will raise an error. Instead, you have to check if an object can respond to a selector at run time using the aptly named **respondsToSelector:** method. It simply returns **YES** or **NO** depending on whether the object can perform the selector:

```
SEL methodToCall = @selector(sayHello);
if ([joe respondsToSelector:methodToCall]) {
    [joe performSelector:methodToCall];
} else {
    NSLog(@"Joe doesn't know how to perform %@.",
        NSStringFromSelector(methodToCall));
}
```

If your selectors are being dynamically generated (e.g., if **methodToCall** is selected from a list of options) or you don't have control over the target object (e.g., **joe** can be one of several different types of objects), it's important to run this check before trying to call **performSelector:**.

Using Selectors

The whole idea behind selectors is to be able to pass around methods just like you pass around objects. This can be used, for example, to dynamically define an "action" for a **Person** object to execute later on in the program. For example, consider the following interface:

Included code sample: Selectors

```
@interface Person : NSObject

@property (copy) NSString *name;
@property (weak) Person *friend;
@property SEL action;

- (void)sayHello;
- (void)sayGoodbye;
- (void)coerceFriend;

@end
```

Along with the corresponding implementation:

```
#import "Person.h"

@implementation Person

@synthesize name = _name;
@synthesize friend = _friend;
@synthesize action = _action;

- (void)sayHello {
    NSLog(@"Hello, says %@.", _name);
}
```

```
- (void)sayGoodbye {
    NSLog(@"Goodbye, says %@.", _name);
}

- (void)coerceFriend {
    NSLog(@"%@ is about to make %@ do something.", _name, [_friend name]);
    [_friend performSelector:_action];
}

@end
```

As you can see, calling the **coerceFriend** method will force a *different* object to perform some arbitrary action. This lets you configure a friendship and a behavior early on in your program and wait for a particular event to occur before triggering the action:

```
#import <Foundation/Foundation.h>
#import "Person.h"

NSString *askUserForAction() {
    // In the real world, this would be capture some
    // user input to determine which method to call.
    NSString *theMethod = @"sayGoodbye";
    return theMethod;
}

int main(int argc, const char * argv[]) {
    @autoreleasepool {

        // Create a person and determine an action to perform.
        Person *joe = [[Person alloc] init];
        joe.name = @"Joe";
        Person *bill = [[Person alloc] init];
        bill.name = @"Bill";
        joe.friend = bill;
        joe.action = NSSelectorFromString(askUserForAction());

        // Wait for an event...

        // Perform the action.
        [joe coerceFriend];

    }
    return 0;
}
```

This is almost exactly how user-interface components in iOS are implemented. For example, if you had a button, you would configure it with a target object (e.g., **friend**), and an action (e.g., **action**). Then, when the user eventually presses the button, it can use **performSelector:** to execute the desired method on the appropriate object. Allowing both the object *and* the method to vary independently affords significant flexibility—the button could literally perform any action with any object without altering the button's class in any way. This also forms the basis of the Target-Action design pattern, which is heavily relied upon in the *iOS Succinctly* companion book.

Summary

In this chapter, we covered instance and class methods, along with some of the most important built-in methods. We worked closely with selectors, which are a way to refer to method names as either source code or strings. We also briefly previewed the Target-Action design pattern, which is an integral aspect of iOS and OS X programming.

The next chapter discusses an alternative way to create private and protected methods in Objective-C.

Chapter 6 Categories and Extensions

Categories are an Objective-C language feature that let you add new methods to an existing class, much like C# extensions. However, do not confuse C# extensions with Objective-C extensions. Objective-C's extensions are a special case of categories that let you define methods that must be declared in the *main implementation block*.

These are powerful features that have many potential uses. First, categories make it possible to split up a class' interface and implementation into several files, which provides much-needed modularity for larger projects. Second, categories let you fix bugs in an existing class (e.g., **NSString**) without the need to subclass it. Third, they provide an effective alternative to the protected and private methods found in C# and other Simula-like languages.

Categories

A **category** is a group of related methods for a class, and all of the methods defined in a category are available through the class as if they were defined in the main interface file. As an example, take the **Person** class that we've been working with throughout this book. If this were a large project, **Person** may have dozens of methods ranging from basic behaviors to interactions with other people to identity checking. The API might call for all of these methods to be available through a single class, but it's much easier for developers to maintain if each group is stored in a separate file. In addition, categories eliminate the need to recompile the entire class every time you change a single method, which can be a time-saver for very large projects.

Let's take a look at how categories can be used to achieve this. We start with a normal class interface and a corresponding implementation:

```
// Person.h
@interface Person : NSObject

@interface Person : NSObject
@property (readonly) NSMutableArray* friends;
@property (copy) NSString* name;

- (void)sayHello;
- (void)sayGoodbye;

@end


// Person.m
#import "Person.h"

@implementation Person

@synthesize name = _name;
@synthesize friends = _friends;
```

```
-(id)init{
    self = [super init];
    if(self){
        _friends = [[NSMutableArray alloc] init];
    }

    return self;
}
- (void)sayHello {
    NSLog(@"Hello, says %@.", _name);
}

- (void)sayGoodbye {
    NSLog(@"Goodbye, says %@.", _name);
}
@end
```

Nothing new here—just a **Person** class with two properties (the `friends` property will be used by our category) and two methods. Next, we'll use a category to store some methods for interacting with other **Person** instances. Create a new file, but instead of a class, use the **Objective-C Category** template. Use **Relations** for the category name and **Person** for the **Category on** field:

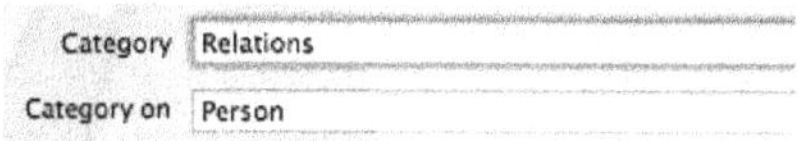

Category	Relations
Category on	Person

Figure 28: Creating the **Person+Relations** *class*

As expected, this will create two files: a header to hold the interface and an implementation. However, these will both look slightly different than what we've been working with. First, let's take a look at the interface:

```
// Person+Relations.h
#import <Foundation/Foundation.h>
#import "Person.h"

@interface Person (Relations)

- (void)addFriend:(Person *)aFriend;
- (void)removeFriend:(Person *)aFriend;
- (void)sayHelloToFriends;

@end
```

Instead of the normal **@interface** declaration, we include the category name in parentheses after the class name we're extending. A category name can be anything, as long as it doesn't conflict with other categories for the same class. A category's *file* name should be the class name followed by a plus sign, followed by the name of the category (e.g., `Person+Relations.h`).

So, this defines our category's interface. Any methods we add in here will be added to the original **Person** class at run time. It will appear as though the **addFriend:**, **removeFriend:**, and **sayHelloToFriends** methods are all defined in **Person.h**, but we can keep our functionality encapsulated and maintainable. Also note that you must import the header for the original class, **Person.h**. The category implementation follows a similar pattern:

```
// Person+Relations.m
#import "Person+Relations.h"

@implementation Person (Relations)

- (void)addFriend:(Person *)aFriend {
    [[self friends] addObject:aFriend];
}

- (void)removeFriend:(Person *)aFriend {
    [[self friends] removeObject:aFriend];
}

- (void)sayHelloToFriends {
    for (Person *friend in [self friends]) {
        NSLog(@"Hello there, %@!", [friend name]);
    }
}

@end
```

This implements all of the methods in **Person+Relations.h**. Just like the category's interface, the category name appears in parentheses after the class name. The category name in the implementation should match the one in the interface.

Also, note that there is no way to define additional properties or instance variables in a category. Categories have to refer back to data stored in the main class (**friends** in this instance).

It's also possible to override the implementation contained in **Person.m** by simply redefining the method in **Person+Relations.m**. This can be used to monkey patch an existing class; however, it's not recommended if you have an alternative solution to the problem, since there would be no way to override the implementation defined by the category. That is to say, unlike the class hierarchy, categories are a flat organizational structure—if you implement the same method in two separate categories, it's impossible for the runtime to figure out which one to use.

The only change you have to make to use a category is to import the category's header file. As you can see in the following example, the **Person** class has access to the methods defined in **Person.h** along with those defined in the category **Person+Relations.h**:

```objc
// main.m
#import <Foundation/Foundation.h>
#import "Person.h"
#import "Person+Relations.h"

int main(int argc, const char * argv[]) {
    @autoreleasepool {
        Person *joe = [[Person alloc] init];
        joe.name = @"Joe";
        Person *bill = [[Person alloc] init];
        bill.name = @"Bill";
        Person *mary = [[Person alloc] init];
        mary.name = @"Mary";

        [joe sayHello];
        [joe addFriend:bill];
        [joe addFriend:mary];
        [joe sayHelloToFriends];
    }
    return 0;
}
```

And that's all there is to creating categories in Objective-C.

Protected Methods

To reiterate, *all* Objective-C methods are public—there is no language construct to mark them as either private or protected. Instead of using "true" protected methods, Objective-C programs can combine categories with the interface/implementation paradigm to achieve the same result.

The idea is simple: declare "protected" methods as a category in a separate header file. This gives subclasses the ability to "opt-in" to the protected methods while unrelated classes use the "public" header file as usual. For example, take a standard **Ship** interface:

```objc
// Ship.h
#import <Foundation/Foundation.h>

@interface Ship : NSObject

- (void)shoot;

@end
```

As we've seen many times, this defines a public method called **shoot**. To declare a *protected* method, we need to create a **Ship** category in a dedicated header file:

```objc
// Ship_Protected.h
#import <Foundation/Foundation.h>
```

```
@interface Ship(Protected)

- (void)prepareToShoot;

@end
```

Any classes that need access to the protected methods (namely, the superclass and any subclasses) can simply import **Ship_Protected.h**. For example, the **Ship** implementation should define a default behavior for the protected method:

```
// Ship.m
#import "Ship.h"
#import "Ship_Protected.h"

@implementation Ship {
    BOOL _gunIsReady;
}

- (void)shoot {
    if (!_gunIsReady) {
        [self prepareToShoot];
        _gunIsReady = YES;
    }
    NSLog(@"Firing!");
}

- (void)prepareToShoot {
    // Execute some private functionality.
    NSLog(@"Preparing the main weapon...");
}
@end
```

Note that if we hadn't imported **Ship_Protected.h**, this **prepareToShoot** implementation would be a private method, as discussed in the Methods chapter. Without a protected category, there would be no way for subclasses to access this method. Let's subclass the **Ship** to see how this works. We'll call it **ResearchShip**:

```
// ResearchShip.h
#import "Ship.h"

@interface ResearchShip : Ship

- (void)extendTelescope;

@end
```

This is a normal subclass interface—it should *not* import the protected header, as this would make the protected methods available to anyone that imports **ResearchShip.h**, which is precisely what we're trying to avoid. Finally, the implementation for the subclass imports the protected methods and (optionally) overrides them:

```
// ResearchShip.m
#import "ResearchShip.h"
#import "Ship_Protected.h"

@implementation ResearchShip

- (void)extendTelescope {
    NSLog(@"Extending the telescope");
}

// Override protected method
- (void)prepareToShoot {
    NSLog(@"Oh shoot! We need to find some weapons!");
}

@end
```

To enforce the protected status of the methods in **Ship_Protected.h**, other classes aren't allowed to import it. They'll just import the normal "public" interfaces of the superclass and subclass:

```
// main.m
#import <Foundation/Foundation.h>
#import "Ship.h"
#import "ResearchShip.h"

int main(int argc, const char * argv[]) {
    @autoreleasepool {

        Ship *genericShip = [[Ship alloc] init];
        [genericShip shoot];

        Ship *discoveryOne = [[ResearchShip alloc] init];
        [discoveryOne shoot];

    }
    return 0;
}
```

Since neither **main.m**, **Ship.h**, nor **ResearchShip.h** import the protected methods, this code won't have access to them. Try adding a **[discoveryOne prepareToShoot]** method—it will throw a compiler error, since the **prepareToShoot** declaration is nowhere to be found.

To summarize, protected methods can be emulated by placing them in a dedicated header file and importing that header file into the implementation files that require access to the protected methods. No other files should import the protected header.

While the workflow presented here is a completely valid organizational tool, keep in mind that Objective-C was never meant to support protected methods. Think of this as an alternative way to structure an Objective-C method, rather than a direct replacement for C#/Simula-style protected methods. It's often better to look for another way to structure your classes rather than forcing your Objective-C code to act like a C# program.

Caveats

One of the biggest issues with categories is that you can't reliably override methods defined in categories for the same class. For example, if you defined an **addFriend:** class in **Person(Relations)** and later decided to change the **addFriend:** implementation via a **Person(Security)** category, there is no way for the runtime to know which method it should use since categories are, by definition, a flat organizational structure. For these kinds of cases, you need to revert to the traditional subclassing paradigm.

Also, it's important to note that a category can't add instance variables. This means you can't declare new properties in a category, as they could only be synthesized in the main implementation. Additionally, while a category technically does have access to its classes' instance variables, it's better practice to access them through their public interface to shield the category from potential changes in the main implementation file.

Extensions

Extensions (also called **class extensions**) are a special type of category that requires their methods to be defined in the *main* implementation block for the associated class, as opposed to an implementation defined in a category. This can be used to override publicly declared property attributes. For example, it is sometimes convenient to change a read-only property to a read-write property within a class' implementation. Consider the normal interface for a **Ship** class:

Included code sample: Extensions

```
// Ship.h
#import <Foundation/Foundation.h>
#import "Person.h"

@interface Ship : NSObject

@property (strong, readonly) Person *captain;

- (id)initWithCaptain:(Person *)captain;

@end
```

It's possible to override the **@property** definition inside of a class extension. This gives you the opportunity to re-declare the property as **readwrite** in the implementation file. Syntactically, an extension looks like an empty category declaration:

```
// Ship.m
#import "Ship.h"


// The class extension.
@interface Ship()

@property (strong, readwrite) Person *captain;

@end


// The standard implementation.
@implementation Ship

@synthesize captain = _captain;

- (id)initWithCaptain:(Person *)captain {
    self = [super init];
    if (self) {
        // This WILL work because of the extension.
        [self setCaptain:captain];
    }
    return self;
}

@end
```

Note the () appended to the class name after the **@interface** directive. This is what marks it as an extension rather than a normal interface or a category. Any properties or methods that appear in the extension *must* be declared in the main implementation block for the class. In this case, we aren't adding any new fields—we're overriding an existing one. But unlike categories, extensions *can* add extra instance variables to a class, which is why we're able to declare properties in a class extension but not a category.

Because we re-declared the **captain** property with a **readwrite** attribute, the **initWithCaptain:** method can use the **setCaptain:** accessor on itself. If you were to delete the extension, the property would return to its read-only status and the compiler would complain. Clients using the **Ship** class aren't supposed to import the implementation file, so the **captain** property will remain read-only.

```
#import <Foundation/Foundation.h>
#import "Person.h"
#import "Ship.h"

int main(int argc, const char * argv[]) {
    @autoreleasepool {

        Person *heywood = [[Person alloc] init];
        heywood.name = @"Heywood";
        Ship *discoveryOne = [[Ship alloc] initWithCaptain:heywood];
```

```
            NSLog(@"%@", [discoveryOne captain].name);

            Person *dave = [[Person alloc] init];
            dave.name = @"Dave";
            // This will NOT work because the property is still read-only.
            [discoveryOne setCaptain:dave];

    }
    return 0;
}
```

Private Methods

Another common use case for extensions is for declaring private methods. In the previous
chapter, we saw how private methods can be declared by simply adding them anywhere in the
implementation file. But, prior to Xcode 4.3, this was not the case. The canonical way to create
a private method was to forward-declare it using a class extension. Let's take a look at this by
slightly altering the **Ship** header from the previous example:

```
// Ship.h
#import <Foundation/Foundation.h>

@interface Ship : NSObject

- (void)shoot;

@end
```

Next, we're going to recreate the example we used when we discussed private methods in the
Methods chapter. Instead of simply adding the private **prepareToShoot** method to the
implementation, we need to forward-declare it in a class extension.

```
// Ship.m
#import "Ship.h"

// The class extension.
@interface Ship()

- (void)prepareToShoot;

@end

// The rest of the implementation.
@implementation Ship {
    BOOL _gunIsReady;
}

- (void)shoot {
    if (!_gunIsReady) {
        [self prepareToShoot];
```

```
        _gunIsReady = YES;
    }
    NSLog(@"Firing!");
}

- (void)prepareToShoot {
    // Execute some private functionality.
    NSLog(@"Preparing the main weapon...");
}

@end
```

The compiler ensures the extension methods are implemented in the main implementation block, which is why it functions as a forward-declaration. Yet because the extension is encapsulated in the implementation file, other objects shouldn't ever know about it, giving us another way to emulate private methods. While newer compilers save you this trouble, it's still important to understand how class extensions work, as it has been a common way to leverage private methods in Objective-C programs until very recently.

Summary

This chapter covered two of the more unique concepts in the Objective-C programming language: categories and extensions. Categories are a way to extend the API of existing classes, and extensions are a way to add *required* methods to the API outside of the main interface file. Both of these were initially designed to ease the burden of maintaining large code bases.

The next chapter continues our journey through Objective-C's organizational structures. We'll learn how to define a protocol, which is an interface that can be implemented by a variety of classes.

Chapter 7 Protocols

In Objective-C, a **protocol** is a group of methods that can be implemented by any class. Protocols are essentially the same as interfaces in C#, and they both have similar goals. They can be used as a pseudo-data type, which is useful for making sure that a dynamically-typed object can respond to a certain set of messages. And, because any class can "adopt" a protocol, they can be used to represent a shared API between completely unrelated classes.

The official documentation discusses both an informal and a formal method for declaring protocols, but informal protocols are really just a unique use of categories and don't provide nearly as many benefits as formal protocols. With this in mind, this chapter focuses solely on *formal* protocols.

Creating a Protocol

First, let's take a look at how to declare a formal protocol. Create a new file in Xcode and select the Objective-C protocol icon under **Mac OS X > Cocoa**:

Figure 29: Xcode icon for protocol files

As usual, this will prompt you for a name. Our protocol will contain methods for calculating the coordinates of an object, so let's call it **CoordinateSupport**:

Figure 30: Naming the protocol

Click **Next** and choose the default location for the file. This will create an empty protocol that looks almost exactly like an interface:

```
// CoordinateSupport.h
#import <Foundation/Foundation.h>

@protocol CoordinateSupport <NSObject>

@end
```

Of course, instead of the **@interface** directive, it uses **@protocol**, followed by the protocol name. The **<NSObject>** syntax lets us incorporate another protocol into **CoordinateSupport**. In this case, we're saying that **CoordinateSupport** also includes all of the methods declared in the **NSObject** protocol (not to be confused with the **NSObject** class).

Next, let's add a few methods and properties to the protocol. This works the same way as declaring methods and properties in an interface:

```
#import <Foundation/Foundation.h>

@protocol CoordinateSupport <NSObject>

@property double x;
@property double y;
@property double z;

- (NSArray *)arrayFromPosition;
- (double)magnitude;

@end
```

Adopting a Protocol

Any class that adopts this protocol is guaranteed to synthesize the x, y, and z properties and implement the **arrayFromPosition** and **magnitude** methods. While this doesn't say *how* they will be implemented, it does give you the opportunity to define a shared API for an arbitrary set of classes.

For example, if we want both **Ship** and **Person** to be able to respond to these properties and methods, we can tell them to adopt the protocol by placing it in angled brackets after the superclass declaration. Also note that, just like using another class, you need to import the protocol file before using it:

```
#import <Foundation/Foundation.h>
#import "CoordinateSupport.h"

@interface Person : NSObject <CoordinateSupport>

@property (copy) NSString *name;
@property (strong) NSMutableSet *friends;

- (void)sayHello;
- (void)sayGoodbye;

@end
```

Now, in addition to the properties and methods defined in this interface, the **Person** class is guaranteed to respond to the API defined by **CoordinateSupport**. Xcode will warn you that the **Person** implementation is incomplete until you synthesize x, y, and z, and implement **arrayFromPosition** and **magnitude**:

```
@implementation Person
        Property 'x' requires method 'setX:' to be defined - use @synthesize, @dynamic or provide a me
@syntl  Property 'x' requires method 'x' to be defined - use @synthesize, @dynamic or provide a methc
@syntl  Property 'y' requires method 'y' to be defined - use @synthesize, @dynamic or provide a metho
        Property 'z' requires method 'setZ:' to be defined - use @synthesize, @dynamic or provide a me
  - (id  Property 'y' requires method 'setY:' to be defined - use @synthesize, @dynamic or provide a me
      se  Incomplete implementation
      i   Property 'z' requires method 'z' to be defined - use @synthesize, @dynamic or provide a metho
          Method in protocol not implemented
```

Figure 31: Incomplete implementation warning for `Person <CoordinateSupport>`

Likewise, a category can adopt a protocol by adding it after the category. For example, to tell the **Person** class to adopt the **CoordinateSupport** protocol in the **Relations** category, you would use the following line:

```
@interface Person(Relations) <CoordinateSupport>
```

And, if your class needs to adopt more than one protocol, you can separate them with commas:

```
@interface Person : NSObject <CoordinateSupport, SomeOtherProtocol>
```

Advantages of Protocols

Without protocols, we would have two options to ensure both **Ship** and **Person** implemented this shared API:

1. Re-declare the exact same properties and methods in both interfaces.
2. Define the API in an abstract superclass and define **Ship** and **Person** as subclasses.

Neither of these options are particularly appealing: the first is redundant and prone to human error, and the second is severely limiting, especially if they already inherit from different parent classes. It should be clear that protocols are much more flexible and reusable, as they shield the API from being dependent on any particular class.

The fact that *any* class can easily adopt a protocol makes it possible to define horizontal relationships on top of an existing class hierarchy:

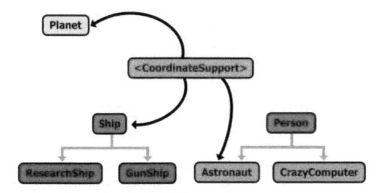

Figure 32: Linking unrelated classes using a protocol

Due to the flexible nature of protocols, the various iOS frameworks make good use of them. For example, user interface controls are often configured using the delegation design pattern, wherein a delegate object is responsible for reacting to user actions. Instead of encapsulating a delegate's responsibilities in an abstract class and forcing delegates to subclass it, iOS defines the necessary API for the delegate in a protocol. This way, it's incredibly easy for *any* object to act as the delegate object. We'll explore this in much more detail in the second half of this series, *iOS Succinctly*.

Protocols as Pseudo-Types

Protocols can be used as psuedo-data types. Instead of making sure a variable is an instance of a class, using a protocol as a type checking tool ensures that the variable always conforms to an arbitrary API. For example, the following **person** variable is guaranteed to implement the CoordinateSupport API.

```
Person <CoordinateSupport> *person = [[Person alloc] init];
```

Still, enforcing protocol adoption is often more useful when used with the **id** data type. This lets you assume certain methods and properties while completely disregarding the object's class.

And of course, the same syntax can be used with a method parameter. The following snippet adds a new **getDistanceFromObject:** method to the API whose parameter is required to conform to **CoordinateSupport** protocol:

```
// CoordinateSupport.h
#import <Foundation/Foundation.h>

@protocol CoordinateSupport <NSObject>
```

```
@property double x;
@property double y;
@property double z;

- (NSArray *)arrayFromPosition;
- (double)magnitude;
- (double)getDistanceFromObject:(id <CoordinateSupport>)theObject;

@end
```

Note that it's entirely possible to use a protocol in the same file as it is defined.

Dynamic Conformance Checking

In addition to the static type checking discussed in the last section, you can also use the conformsToProtocol: method defined by the NSObject protocol to dynamically check whether an object conforms to a protocol or not. This is useful for preventing errors when working with dynamic objects (objects typed as id).

The following example assumes the Person class adopts the CoordinateSupport protocol, while the Ship class does not. It uses a dynamically typed object called mysteryObject to store an instance of Person, and then uses conformsToProtocol: to check if it has coordinate support. If it does, it's safe to use the x, y, and z properties, as well as the other methods declared in the CoordinateSupport protocol:

```
// main.m
#import <Foundation/Foundation.h>
#import "Person.h"
#import "Ship.h"

int main(int argc, const char * argv[]) {
    @autoreleasepool {
        id mysteryObject = [[Person alloc] init];
        [mysteryObject setX:10.0];
        [mysteryObject setY:0.0];
        [mysteryObject setZ:7.5];

        // Uncomment next line to see the "else" portion of conditional.
        //mysteryObject = [[Ship alloc] init];

        if ([mysteryObject
             conformsToProtocol:@protocol(CoordinateSupport)]) {
            NSLog(@"Ok to assume coordinate support.");
            NSLog(@"The object is located at (%0.2f, %0.2f, %0.2f)",
                  [mysteryObject x],
                  [mysteryObject y],
                  [mysteryObject z]);
        } else {
            NSLog(@"Error: Not safe to assume coordinate support.");
            NSLog(@"I have no idea where that object is...");
        }
```

```
    }
    return 0;
}
```

If you uncomment the line that reassigns the **mysteryObject** to a **Ship** instance, the **conformsToProtocol:** method will return **NO**, and you won't be able to safely use the API defined by **CoordinateSupport**. If you're not sure what kind of object a variable will hold, this kind of dynamic protocol checking is important to prevent your program from crashing when you try to call a method that doesn't exist.

Also notice the new **@protocol()** directive. This works much like **@selector()**, except instead of a method name, it takes a protocol name. It returns a **Protocol** object, which can be passed to **conformsToProtocol:**, among other built-in methods. The protocol header file does *not* need to be imported for **@protocol()** to work.

Forward-Declaring Protocols

If you end up working with a lot of protocols, you'll eventually run into a situation where two protocols rely on one another. This circular relationship poses a problem for the compiler, since it cannot successfully import either of them without the other. For example, let's say we were trying to abstract out some GPS functionality into a **GPSSupport** protocol, but want to be able to convert between the "normal" coordinates of our existing **CoordinateSupport** and the coordinates used by **GPSSupport**. The **GPSSupport** protocol is pretty simple:

```
#import <Foundation/Foundation.h>
#import "CoordinateSupport.h"

@protocol GPSSupport <NSObject>

- (void)copyCoordinatesFromObject:(id <CoordinateSupport>)theObject;

@end
```

This doesn't pose any problems, that is, until we need to reference the **GPSSupport** protocol from **CoordinateSupport.h**:

```
#import <Foundation/Foundation.h>
#import "GPSSupport.h"

@protocol CoordinateSupport <NSObject>

@property double x;
@property double y;
@property double z;
```

```
- (NSArray *)arrayFromPosition;
- (double)magnitude;
- (double)getDistanceFromObject:(id <CoordinateSupport>)theObject;

- (void)copyGPSCoordinatesFromObject:(id <GPSSupport>)theObject;

@end
```

Now, the **CoordinateSupport.h** file requires the **GPSSupport.h** file to compile correctly, and vice versa. It's a chicken-or-the-egg kind of problem, and the compiler will not like it very much:

> ⓘ Cannot find protocol declaration for 'CoordinateSupport'

Figure 33: Compiler error caused by circular protocol references

Resolving the recursive relationship is simple. All you need to do is forward-declare one of the protocols instead of trying to import it directly:

```
#import <Foundation/Foundation.h>

@protocol CoordinateSupport;

@protocol GPSSupport <NSObject>

- (void)copyCoordinatesFromObject:(id <CoordinateSupport>)theObject;

@end
```

All **@protocol CoordinateSupport;** says is that **CoordinateSupport** is indeed a protocol and the compiler can assume it exists without importing it. Note the semicolon at the end of the statement. This could be done in either of the two protocols; the point is to remove the circular reference. The compiler doesn't care how you do it.

Summary

Protocols are an incredibly powerful feature of Objective-C. They let you capture relationships between arbitrary classes when it's not feasible to connect them with a common parent class. We'll utilize several built-in protocols in **iOS Succinctly**, as many of the core functions of an iPhone or iPad app are defined as protocols.

The next chapter introduces exceptions and errors, two very important tools for managing the problems that inevitably arise while writing Objective-C programs.

Chapter 8 Exceptions and Errors

In Objective-C, there are two types of errors that can occur while a program is running. *Unexpected* errors are "serious" programming errors that typically cause your program to exit prematurely. These are called **exceptions**, since they represent an exceptional condition in your program. On the other hand, *expected* errors occur naturally in the course of a program's execution and can be used to determine the success of an operation. These are referred to as **errors**.

You can also approach the distinction between exceptions and errors as a difference in their target audiences. In general, exceptions are used to inform the *programmer* about something that went wrong, while errors are used to inform the *user* that a requested action could not be completed.

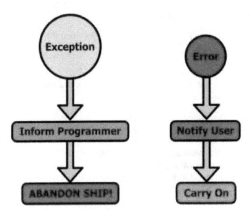

Figure 34: Control flow for exceptions and errors

For example, trying to access an array index that doesn't exist is an exception (a programmer error), while failing to open a file is an error (a user error). In the former case, something likely went very wrong in the flow of your program and it should probably shut down soon after the exception. In the latter, you would want to tell the user that the file couldn't be opened and possibly ask to retry the action, but there is no reason your program wouldn't be able to keep running after the error.

Exception Handling

The main benefit to Objective-C's exception handling capabilities is the ability to separate the handling of errors from the detection of errors. When a portion of code encounters an exception, it can "throw" it to the nearest error handling block, which can "catch" specific exceptions and handle them appropriately. The fact that exceptions can be thrown from arbitrary locations eliminates the need to constantly check for success or failure messages from each function involved in a particular task.

The **@try**, **@catch()**, and **@finally** compiler directives are used to catch and handle exceptions, and the **@throw** directive is used to detect them. If you've worked with exceptions in C#, these exception handling constructs should be familiar to you.

It's important to note that in Objective-C, exceptions are relatively slow. As a result, their use should be limited to catching serious programming errors—not for basic control flow. If you're trying to determine what to do based on an *expected* error (e.g., failing to load a file), please refer to the <u>Error Handling</u> section.

The NSException Class

Exceptions are represented as instances of the **NSException** class or a subclass thereof. This is a convenient way to encapsulate all the necessary information associated with an exception. The three properties that constitute an exception are described as follows:

- **name** – An instance of **NSString** that uniquely identifies the exception.
- **reason** – An instance of **NSString** containing a human-readable description of the exception.
- **userInfo** – An instance of **NSDictionary** that contains application-specific information related to the exception.

The Foundation framework defines several constants that define the "standard" <u>exception names</u>. These strings can be used to check what type of exception was caught.

You can also use the **initWithName:reason:userInfo:** initialization method to create new exception objects with your own values. Custom exception objects can be caught and thrown using the same methods covered in the upcoming sections.

Generating Exceptions

Let's start by taking a look at the default exception-handling behavior of a program. The **objectAtIndex:** method of **NSArray** is defined to throw an **NSRangeException** (a subclass of **NSException**) when you try to access an index that doesn't exist. So, if you request the 10th item of an array that has only three elements, you'll have yourself an exception to experiment with:

```
#import <Foundation/Foundation.h>

int main(int argc, const char * argv[]) {
    @autoreleasepool {

        NSArray *crew = [NSArray arrayWithObjects:
                            @"Dave",
                            @"Heywood",
                            @"Frank", nil];

        // This will throw an exception.
```

```
        NSLog(@"%@", [crew objectAtIndex:10]);

    }
    return 0;
}
```

When it encounters an uncaught exception, Xcode halts the program and points you to the line that caused the problem.

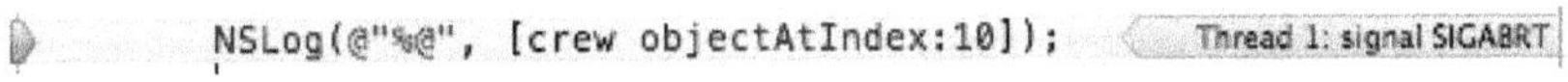

NSLog(@"%@", [crew objectAtIndex:10]);   Thread 1: signal SIGABRT

Figure 35: Aborting a program due to an uncaught exception

Next, we'll learn how to catch exceptions and prevent the program from terminating.

Catching Exceptions

To handle an exception, any code that *may* result in an exception should be placed in a **@try** block. Then, you can catch specific exceptions using the **@catch()** directive. If you need to execute any housekeeping code, you can optionally place it in a **@finally** block. The following example shows all three of these exception-handling directives:

```
@try {
    NSLog(@"%@", [crew objectAtIndex:10]);
}
@catch (NSException *exception) {
    NSLog(@"Caught an exception");
    // We'll just silently ignore the exception.
}
@finally {
    NSLog(@"Cleaning up");
}
```

This should output the following in your Xcode console:

```
Caught an exception!
Name: NSRangeException
Reason: *** -[__NSArrayI objectAtIndex:]: index 10 beyond bounds [0 .. 2]
Cleaning up
```

When the program encounters the [crew objectAtIndex:10] message, it throws an **NSRangeException**, which is caught in the **@catch()** directive. Inside of the **@catch()** block is where the exception is actually handled. In this case, we just display a descriptive error message, but in most cases, you'll probably want to write some code to take care of the problem.

When an exception is encountered in the **@try** block, the program jumps to the corresponding **@catch()** block, which means any code *after* the exception occurred won't be executed. This poses a problem if the **@try** block needs some cleaning up (e.g., if it opened a file, that file needs to be closed). The **@finally** block solves this problem, since it is *guaranteed* to be executed regardless of whether an exception occurred. This makes it the perfect place to tie up any loose ends from the **@try** block.

Catching Custom Objects

The parentheses after the **@catch()** directive let you define what type of exception you're trying to catch. In this case, it's an **NSException**, which is the standard exception class. But, an exception can actually be *any* class—not just an **NSException**. For example, the following **@catch()** directive will handle a generic object:

```
@catch (id genericException)
```

We'll learn how to throw instances of **NSException** as well as generic objects in the next section.

Throwing Exceptions

When you detect an exceptional condition in your code, you create an instance of **NSException** and populate it with the relevant information. Then, you throw it using the aptly named **@throw** directive, prompting the nearest **@try/@catch** block to handle it.

For example, the following example defines a function for generating random numbers between a specified interval. If the caller passes an invalid interval, the function throws a custom error.

```
#import <Foundation/Foundation.h>

int generateRandomInteger(int minimum, int maximum) {
    if (minimum >= maximum) {
        // Create the exception.
        NSException *exception = [NSException
            exceptionWithName:@"RandomNumberIntervalException"
            reason:@"*** generateRandomInteger(): "
                    "maximum parameter not greater than minimum parameter"
            userInfo:nil];

        // Throw the exception.
        @throw exception;
    }
    // Return a random integer.
    return arc4random_uniform((maximum - minimum) + 1) + minimum;
}

int main(int argc, const char * argv[]) {
    @autoreleasepool {

        int result = 0;
        @try {
            result = generateRandomInteger(0, 10);
```

```
        }
        @catch (NSException *exception) {
            NSLog(@"Problem!!! Caught exception: %@", [exception name]);
        }

        NSLog(@"Random Number: %i", result);

    }
    return 0;
}
```

Since this code passes a valid interval (`0, 10`) to `generateRandomInteger()`, it won't have an exception to catch. However, if you change the interval to something like (`0, -10`), you'll get to see the `@catch()` block in action. This is essentially what's going on under the hood when the framework classes encounter exceptions (e.g., the **NSRangeException** raised by **NSArray**).

Re-Throwing Exceptions

It's also possible to re-throw exceptions that you've already caught. This is useful if you want to be informed that a particular exception occurred but don't necessarily want to handle it yourself. As a convenience, you can even omit the argument to the `@throw` directive:

```
@try {
    result = generateRandomInteger(0, -10);
}
@catch (NSException *exception) {
    NSLog(@"Problem!!! Caught exception: %@", [exception name]);

    // Re-throw the current exception.
    @throw
}
```

This passes the caught exception up to the next-highest handler, which in this case is the top-level exception handler. This should display the output from our `@catch()` block, as well as the default **Terminating app due to uncaught exception...** message, followed by an abrupt exit.

Throwing Custom Objects

The `@throw` directive isn't limited to **NSException** objects—it can throw literally *any* object. The following example throws an **NSNumber** object instead of a normal exception. Also notice how you can target different objects by adding multiple `@catch()` statements after the `@try` block:

```
#import <Foundation/Foundation.h>

int generateRandomInteger(int minimum, int maximum) {
    if (minimum >= maximum) {
        // Generate a number using "default" interval.
        NSNumber *guess = [NSNumber
```

```
                        numberWithInt:generateRandomInteger(0, 10)];

        // Throw the number.
        @throw guess;
    }
    // Return a random integer.
    return arc4random_uniform((maximum - minimum) + 1) + minimum;
}

int main(int argc, const char * argv[]) {
    @autoreleasepool {

        int result = 0;
        @try {
            result = generateRandomInteger(30, 10);
        }
        @catch (NSNumber *guess) {
            NSLog(@"Warning: Used default interval");
            result = [guess intValue];
        }
        @catch (NSException *exception) {
            NSLog(@"Problem!!! Caught exception: %@", [exception name]);
        }

        NSLog(@"Random Number: %i", result);

    }
    return 0;
}
```

Instead of throwing an **NSException** object, **generateRandomInteger()** tries to generate a new number between some "default" bounds. The example shows you how **@throw** can work with different types of objects, but strictly speaking, this isn't the best application design, nor is it the most efficient use of Objective-C's exception-handling tools. If you really were just planning on using the thrown value like the previous code does, you would be better off with a plain old conditional check using **NSError**, as discussed in the next section.

In addition, some of Apple's core frameworks *expect* an **NSException** object to be thrown, so be careful with custom objects when integrating with the standard libraries.

Error Handling

Whereas exceptions are designed to let programmers know when things have gone fatally wrong, errors are designed to be an efficient, straightforward way to check if an action succeeded or not. Unlike exceptions, errors *are* designed to be used in your everyday control flow statements.

The NSError Class

The one thing that errors and exceptions have in common is that they are both implemented as objects. The **NSError** class encapsulates all of the necessary information for representing errors:

- **code** – An **NSInteger** that represents the error's unique identifier.

- **domain** – An instance of **NSString** defining the domain for the error (described in more detail in the next section).

- **userInfo** – An instance of **NSDictionary** that contains application-specific information related to the error. This is typically used much more than the **userInfo** dictionary of **NSException**.

In addition to these core attributes, **NSError** also stores several values designed to aid in the rendering and processing of errors. All of these are actually shortcuts into the **userInfo** dictionary described in the previous list.

- **localizedDescription** – An **NSString** containing the full description of the error, which typically includes the reason for the failure. This value is typically displayed to the user in an alert panel.

- **localizedFailureReason** – An **NSString** containing a stand-alone description of the reason for the error. This is only used by clients that want to isolate the reason for the error from its full description.

- **recoverySuggestion** – An **NSString** instructing the user how to recover from the error.

- **localizedRecoveryOptions** – An **NSArray** of titles used for the buttons of the error dialog. If this array is empty, a single **OK** button is displayed to dismiss the alert.

- **helpAnchor** – An **NSString** to display when the user presses the **Help** anchor button in an alert panel.

As with **NSException**, the **initWithDomain:code:userInfo** method can be used to initialize custom **NSError** instances.

Error Domains

An error domain is like a namespace for error codes. Codes should be unique within a single domain, but they can overlap with codes from other domains. In addition to preventing code collisions, domains also provide information about where the error is coming from. The four main built-in error domains are: **NSMachErrorDomain**, **NSPOSIXErrorDomain**, **NSOSStatusErrorDomain**, and **NSCocoaErrorDomain**. The **NSCocoaErrorDomain** contains the error codes for many of Apple's standard Objective-C frameworks; however, there are some frameworks that define their own domains (e.g., **NSXMLParserErrorDomain**).

If you need to create custom error codes for your libraries and applications, you should always add them to *your own* error domain—never extend any of the built-in domains. Creating your own domain is a relatively trivial job. Because domains are just strings, all you have to do is define a string constant that doesn't conflict with any of the other error domains in your

application. Apple suggests that domains take the form of
`com.<company>.<project>.ErrorDomain`.

Capturing Errors

There are no dedicated language constructs for handling **NSError** instances (though several built-in classes are designed to handle them). They are designed to be used in conjunction with specially designed functions that return an object when they succeed and **nil** when they fail. The general procedure for capturing errors is as follows:

1. Declare an **NSError** variable. You don't need to allocate or initialize it.

2. Pass that variable as a double pointer to a function that *may* result in an error. If anything goes wrong, the function will use this reference to record information about the error.

3. Check the return value of that function for success or failure. If the operation failed, you can use **NSError** to handle the error yourself or display it to the user.

As you can see, a function doesn't typically *return* an **NSError** object—it returns whatever value it's supposed to if it succeeds, otherwise it returns **nil**. You should always use the return value of a function to detect errors—never use the presence or absence of an **NSError** object to check if an action succeeded. Error objects are only supposed to describe a potential error, not tell you if one occurred.

The following example demonstrates a realistic use case for **NSError**. It uses a file-loading method of **NSString**, which is actually outside the scope of the book. The *iOS Succinctly* book covers file management in depth, but for now, let's just focus on the error-handling capabilities of Objective-C.

First, we generate a file path pointing to **~/Desktop/SomeContent.txt.** Then, we create an **NSError** reference and pass it to the **stringWithContentsOfFile:encoding:error:** method to capture information about any errors that occur while loading the file. Note that we're passing a *reference* to the ***error** pointer, which means the method is requesting a pointer to a pointer (i.e. a double pointer). This makes it possible for the method to populate the variable with its own content. Finally, we check the *return value* (not the existence of the **error** variable) to see if **stringWithContentsOfFile:encoding:error:** succeeded or not. If it did, it's safe to work with the value stored in the **content** variable; otherwise, we use the **error** variable to display information about what went wrong.

```
#import <Foundation/Foundation.h>

int main(int argc, const char * argv[]) {
    @autoreleasepool {

        // Generate the desired file path.
        NSString *filename = @"SomeContent.txt";
        NSArray *paths = NSSearchPathForDirectoriesInDomains(
                        NSDesktopDirectory, NSUserDomainMask, YES
                    );
        NSString *desktopDir = [paths objectAtIndex:0];
        NSString *path = [desktopDir
                        stringByAppendingPathComponent:filename];
```

```
// Try to load the file.
NSError *error;
NSString *content = [NSString stringWithContentsOfFile:path
                             encoding:NSUTF8StringEncoding
                             error:&error];

// Check if it worked.
if (content == nil) {
    // Some kind of error occurred.
    NSLog(@"Error loading file %@!", path);
    NSLog(@"Description: %@", [error localizedDescription]);
    NSLog(@"Reason: %@", [error localizedFailureReason]);
} else {
    // Content loaded successfully.
    NSLog(@"Content loaded!");
    NSLog(@"%@", content);
}
}
return 0;
}
```

Since the **~/Desktop/SomeContent.txt** file probably doesn't exist on your machine, this code will most likely result in an error. All you have to do to make the load succeed is create **SomeContent.txt** on your desktop.

Custom Errors

Custom errors can be configured by accepting a double pointer to an **NSError** object and populating it on your own. Remember that your function or method should return either an object or **nil**, depending on whether it succeeds or fails (do not return the **NSError** reference).

The next example uses an error instead of an exception to mitigate invalid parameters in the **generateRandomInteger()** function. Notice that ****error** is a double pointer, which lets us populate the underlying variable from within the function. It's very important to check that the user actually passed a valid ****error** parameter with **if (error != NULL)**. You should always do this in your own error-generating functions. Since the ****error** parameter is a double pointer, we can assign a value to the underlying variable via ***error**. And again, we check for errors using the *return value* (**if (result == nil)**), not the **error** variable.

```
#import <Foundation/Foundation.h>

NSNumber *generateRandomInteger(int minimum, int maximum, NSError **error) {
    if (minimum >= maximum) {
        if (error != NULL) {

            // Create the error.
            NSString *domain = @"com.MyCompany.RandomProject.ErrorDomain";
            int errorCode = 4;
            NSMutableDictionary *userInfo = [NSMutableDictionary dictionary];
```

```
               [userInfo setObject:@"Maximum parameter is not greater than minimum
parameter"
                       forKey:NSLocalizedDescriptionKey];

           // Populate the error reference.
           *error = [[NSError alloc] initWithDomain:domain
                                        code:errorCode
                                    userInfo:userInfo];
       }
       return nil;
   }
   // Return a random integer.
   return [NSNumber
           numberWithInt:arc4random_uniform((maximum - minimum) + 1) + minimum];
}

int main(int argc, const char * argv[]) {
   @autoreleasepool {

       NSError *error;
       NSNumber *result = generateRandomInteger(0, -10, &error);

       if (result == nil) {
           // Check to see what went wrong.
           NSLog(@"An error occurred!");
           NSLog(@"Domain: %@ Code: %li", [error domain], [error code]);
           NSLog(@"Description: %@", [error localizedDescription]);
       } else {
           // Safe to use the returned value.
           NSLog(@"Random Number: %i", [result intValue]);
       }

   }
   return 0;
}
```

All of the **localizedDescription**, **localizedFailureReason**, and related properties of
NSError are actually stored in its **userInfo** dictionary using special keys defined by
NSLocalizedDescriptionKey, **NSLocalizedFailureReasonErrorKey**, etc. So, all we have to
do to describe the error is add some strings to the appropriate keys, as shown in the last
sample.

Typically, you'll want to define constants for custom error domains and codes so that they are
consistent across classes.

Summary

This chapter provided a detailed discussion of the differences between exceptions and errors.
Exceptions are designed to inform programmers of fatal problems in their program, whereas
errors represent a failed user action. Generally, a production-ready application should *not* throw

exceptions, except in the case of truly exceptional circumstances (e.g., running out of memory in a device).

We covered the basic usage of `NSError`, but keep in mind that there are several built-in classes dedicated to processing and displaying errors. Unfortunately, these are all graphical components, and thus outside the scope of this book. The *iOS Succinctly* sequel has a dedicated section on displaying and recovering from errors.

In the final chapter of *Objective-C Succinctly*, we'll discuss one of the more confusing topics in Objective-C. We'll discover how blocks let us treat *functionality* the same way we treat *data*. This will have a far-reaching impact on what's possible in an Objective-C application.

Chapter 9 Blocks

Blocks are actually an extension to the C programming language, but they are heavily utilized by Apple's Objective-C frameworks. They are similar to C#'s lambdas in that they let you define a block of statements inline and pass it around to other functions as if it were an object.

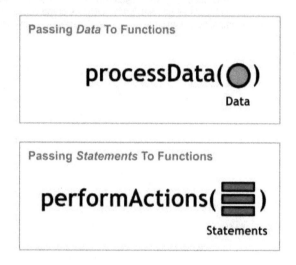

Figure 36: Processing data with functions vs. performing arbitrary actions with blocks

Blocks are incredibly convenient for defining callback methods since they let you define the desired functionality at the point of invocation rather than somewhere else in your program. In addition, blocks are implemented as **closures** (just like lambdas in C#), which makes it possible to capture the local state surrounding the block without any extra work.

Creating Blocks

Block syntax can be a little unsettling compared to the Objective-C syntax we've been using throughout this book, so don't worry if it takes a while to be comfortable with them. We'll start by looking at a simple example:

```
^(int x) {
    return x * 2;
};
```

This defines a block that takes an integer parameter, x, and returns that value multiplied by two. Aside from the caret (^), this resembles a normal function: it has a parameter list in parentheses, an instruction block enclosed in curly braces, and an (optional) return value. In C#, this is written as:

```
x => x * 2;
```

But, blocks aren't limited to simple expressions—they can contain an arbitrary number of statements, just like a function. For example, you can add an NSLog() call before returning a value:

```
^(int x) {
    NSLog(@"About to multiply %i by 2.", x);
    return x * 2;
};
```

Parameter-less Blocks

If your block doesn't take any parameters, you can omit the parameter list altogether:

```
^ {
    NSLog(@"This is a pretty contrived block.");
    NSLog(@"It just outputs these two messages.");
};
```

Using Blocks as Callbacks

On its own, a block isn't all that useful. Typically, you'll pass them to another method as a callback function. This is a very powerful language feature, as it lets you treat *functionality* as a parameter, rather than being limited to *data*. You can pass a block to a method as you would any other literal value:

```
[anObject doSomethingWithBlock:^(int x) {
    NSLog(@"Multiplying %i by two");
    return x * 2;
}];
```

The **doSomethingWithBlock:** implementation can run the block just like it would run a function, which opens the door to a lot of new organizational paradigms.

As a more practical example, let's take a look at the **sortUsingComparator:** method defined by **NSMutableArray**. This provides the exact same functionality as the **sortedArrayUsingFunction:** method we used in the Data Types chapter, except you define the sort algorithm in a block instead of a full-fledged function:

Included code sample: SortUsingBlock

```
#import <Foundation/Foundation.h>

int main(int argc, const char * argv[]) {
    @autoreleasepool {

        NSMutableArray *numbers = [NSMutableArray arrayWithObjects:
                                    [NSNumber numberWithFloat:3.0f],
                                    [NSNumber numberWithFloat:5.5f],
                                    [NSNumber numberWithFloat:1.0f],
                                    [NSNumber numberWithFloat:12.2f], nil];

        [numbers
         sortUsingComparator:^NSComparisonResult(id obj1, id obj2) {
            float number1 = [obj1 floatValue];
            float number2 = [obj2 floatValue];
            if (number1 < number2) {
                return NSOrderedAscending;
            } else if (number1 > number2) {
                return NSOrderedDescending;
            } else {
                return NSOrderedSame;
            }
        }];

        for (int i=0; i<[numbers count]; i++) {
            NSLog(@"%i: %0.1f", i, [[numbers objectAtIndex:i] floatValue]);
        }

    }
    return 0;
}
```

Again, this is a straightforward ascending sort, but being able to define the sort algorithm in the same place as the function invocation is more intuitive than having to define an independent function elsewhere in the program. Also notice that you can declare local variables in a block just as you would in a function.

The standard Objective-C frameworks use this design pattern for everything from sorting, to enumeration, to animation. In fact, you could even replace the for-loop in the last example with **NSArray**'s **enumerateObjectsUsingBlock:** method, as shown here:

```
[sortedNumbers
 enumerateObjectsUsingBlock:^(id obj, NSUInteger idx, BOOL *stop) {
    NSLog(@"%lu: %0.1f", idx, [obj floatValue]);
    if (idx == 2) {
        // Stop enumerating at the end of this iteration.
        *stop = YES;
    }
}];
```

The **obj** parameter is the current object, **idx** is the current index, and ***stop** is a way to exit the enumeration prematurely. Setting the ***stop** pointer to **YES** tells the method to stop enumerating after the current iteration. All of this behavior is specified by the **enumerateObjectsUsingBlock:** method.

While animation is a bit off-topic for this book, it's still worth a brief explanation to help understand the utility of blocks. **UIView** is one of the most used classes in iOS programming. It's a generic graphical container that lets you animate its contents via the **animateWithDuration:animations:** method. The second parameter is a block that defines the final state of the animation, and the method automatically figures out how to animate the properties using the first parameter. This is an elegant, user-friendly way to define transitions and other timer-based behavior. We'll discuss animations in much more detail in the upcoming *iOS Succinctly* book.

Storing and Executing Blocks

Aside from passing them to methods, blocks can also be stored in variables for later use. This use case essentially serves as an alternative way to define functions:

```
#import <Foundation/Foundation.h>

int main(int argc, const char * argv[]) {
    @autoreleasepool {

        int (^addIntegers)(int, int);

        addIntegers = ^(int x, int y) {
            return x + y;
        };

        int result = addIntegers(24, 18);
        NSLog(@"%i", result);

    }
    return 0;
}
```

First, let's inspect the syntax for declaring block variables: **int (^addIntegers)(int, int)**. The name of this variable is simply **addIntegers** (without the caret). This can be confusing if you haven't been using blocks very long. It helps to think of the caret as the block's version of the dereference operator (*). For example, a *pointer* called **addIntegers** would be declared as ***addIntegers**—likewise, a *block* of the same name is declared as **^addIntegers**. However, keep in mind that this is merely a superficial similarity.

In addition to the variable name, you also need to declare all of the metadata associated with the block: the number of parameters, their types, and the return type. This enables the compiler to enforce type safety with block variables. Note that the caret is *not* part of the variable name—it's only required in the declaration.

Next, we use the standard assignment operator (=) to store a block in the variable. Of course, the block's parameters (`(int x, int y)`) must match parameter types declared by the variable (`(int, int)`). A semicolon is also required after the block definition, just like a normal variable assignment. Once it has been populated with a value, the variable can be called just like a function: `addIntegers(24, 18)`.

Parameter-less Block Variables

If your block doesn't take any parameters, you must explicitly declare this in the variable by placing **void** in the parameter list:

```
void (^contrived)(void) = ^ {
    NSLog(@"This is a pretty contrived block.");
    NSLog(@"It just outputs these two messages.");
};

contrived();
```

Working with Variables

Variables inside of blocks behave in much the same way as they do in normal functions. You can create local variables within the block, access parameters passed to the block, and use global variables and functions (e.g., **NSLog()**). But, blocks also have access to **non-local variables**, which are variables from the enclosing lexical scope.

```
int initialValue = 32;
int (^addToInitialValue)(int) = ^(int x) {
    return initialValue + x;
};

NSLog(@"%i", addToInitialValue(10)); // 42
```

In this case, `initialValue` is considered a non-local variable within the block because it is defined outside of the block (*not* locally, relative to the block). Of course, the fact that non-local variables are read-only implies that you cannot assign to them:

```
int initialValue = 32;
int (^addToInitialValue)(int) = ^(int x) {
    initialValue = 5; // This will throw a compiler error.
    return initialValue + x;
};
```

Having access to the surrounding (non-local) variables is a big deal when using inline blocks as method parameters. It provides a convenient way to represent any state required within the block.

For example, if you were animating the color of a UI component and the target color was calculated and stored in a local variable before the block definition, you could simply use the local variable within the block—no extra work required. If you didn't have access to non-local variables, you would have passed the color value as an additional block parameter. When your callback functionality relies on a large portion of the surrounding state, this can be very cumbersome.

Blocks Are Closures

However, blocks don't just have *access* to non-local variables—they also ensure that those variables will *never* change, no matter when or where the block is executed. In most programming languages, this is called a **closure**.

Closures work by making a constant, read-only copy of any non-local variables and storing them in a **reference table** with the statements that make up the block itself. These read-only values are used every time the block is executed, which means that even if the original non-local variable changes, the value used by the block is guaranteed to be the same as it was when the block was defined.

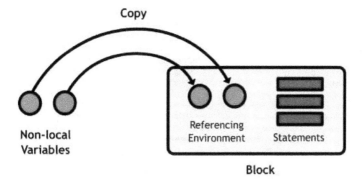

Figure 37: Storing non-local variables in a reference table

We can see this in action by assigning a new value to the `initialValue` variable from the previous example:

```
int initialValue = 32;
int (^addToInitialValue)(int) = ^(int x) {
    return initialValue + x;
};

NSLog(@"%i", addToInitialValue(10)); // 42

initialValue = 100;
```

```
NSLog(@"%i", addToInitialValue(10)); // Still 42.
```

No matter where you call **addToInitialValue()**, the **initialValue** used by the block will *always* be **32**, because that's what it was when it was created. For all intents and purposes, it's as though the **initialValue** variable was transformed into a literal value inside of the block.

So, the utility of blocks is two-fold:

1. They allow you to represent functionality as an object.
2. They let you represent state information alongside that functionality.

The whole idea behind encapsulating functionality in a block is to be able to use it *later* in the program. Closures make it possible to ensure predictable behavior *whenever* a block is executed by freezing the surrounding state. This makes them an integral aspect of block programming.

Mutable Block Variables

For most cases, capturing state with closures is intuitively what you would expect from a block. There are, however, times that call for the opposite behavior. **Mutable block variables** are non-local variables that are designated read-write instead of the default read-only. To make a non-local variable mutable, you have to declare it with the **__block** modifier, which creates a direct link between the variable used outside the block and the one used inside of the block. This opens the door to using blocks as iterators, generators, and any other kind of object that processes state.

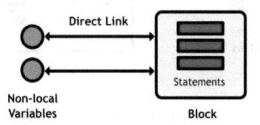

Figure 38: Creating a direct link with a mutable block variable

The following example shows you how to make a non-local variable mutable:

```
#import <Foundation/Foundation.h>
#import "Person.h"

int main(int argc, const char * argv[]) {
    @autoreleasepool {

        __block NSString *name = @"Dave";
```

```
    void (^generateRandomName)(void) = ^ {
        NSLog(@"Changing %@ to Frank", name);
        name = @"Frank";
    };

    NSLog(@"%@", name);           // Dave

    // Change it from inside the block.
    generateRandomName();         // Changing Dave to Frank.
    NSLog(@"%@", name);           // Frank

    // Change it from outside the block.
    name = @"Heywood";
    generateRandomName();         // Changing Heywood to Frank.

    }
    return 0;
}
```

This looks almost exactly the same as the previous example, with two very significant differences. First, the non-local **name** variable *can* be assigned from within the block. Second, changing the variable outside of the block *does* update the value used within the block. It's even possible to create multiple blocks that all manipulate the same non-local variable.

The only caveat to using the __block modifier is that it *cannot* be used on variable-length arrays.

Defining Methods that Accept Blocks

Arguably, creating methods that accept blocks is more useful than storing them in local variables. It gives you the opportunity to add your own **enumerateObjectsUsingBlock:**-style methods to custom classes.

Consider the following interface for the **Person** class:

```
// Person.h
@interface Person : NSObject

@property int age;

- (void)celebrateBirthdayWithBlock:(void (^)(int))activity;

@end
```

The **void (^)(int)** code is the data type for the block that you want to accept. In this case, we'll be accepting a block with no return value and a single integer parameter. Notice that, unlike block variables, this doesn't require a name for the block—just an unadorned ^ character.

You now have all the skills necessary to create methods that accept blocks as parameters. A simple implementation for the **Person** interface shown in the previous example might look something like:

```
// Person.m
#import "Person.h"

@implementation Person

@synthesize age = _age;

- (void)celebrateBirthdayWithBlock:(void (^)(int))activity {
    NSLog(@"It's a party!!!");
    activity(self.age);
}

@end
```

Then, you can pass a customizable activity to perform on a **Person**'s birthday like so:

```
// main.m
int main(int argc, const char * argv[]) {
    @autoreleasepool {

        Person *dave = [[Person alloc] init];
        dave.age = 37;

        [dave celebrateBirthdayWithBlock:^(int age) {
            NSLog(@"Woot! I'm turning %i", age + 1);
        }];

    }
    return 0;
}
```

It should be readily apparent that using blocks as parameters is infinitely more flexible than the standard data types we've been using up until this chapter. You can actually tell an instance to *do* something, rather than merely process data.

Summary

Blocks let you represent statements as Objective-C objects, which enables you to pass arbitrary *actions* to a function instead of being limited to *data*. This is useful for everything from iterating over a sequence of objects to animating UI components. Blocks are a versatile extension to the C programming language, and they are a necessary tool if you're planning to do a lot of work with the standard iOS frameworks. In this chapter, we learned how to create, store, and execute blocks, and we learned about the intricacies of closures and the **__block** storage modifier. We also discussed some common usage paradigms for blocks.

Conclusion

Thus concludes our journey through Objective-C. We've covered everything from basic syntax to core data types, classes, protocols, properties, methods, memory management, error handling, and even the advanced use of blocks. We focused more on language features than creating graphical applications, but this provided a solid foundation for iOS app development. By now, I hope you're feeling very comfortable with the Objective-C language.

Remember that Objective-C relies on many of the same object-oriented concepts as other OOP languages. While we only touched on a few object-oriented design patterns in this book, virtually all of the organizational paradigms available to other languages are also possible in Objective-C. This means that you can easily leverage your existing object-oriented knowledge base with the tools presented in the preceding chapters.

iOS Succinctly

If you're ready to start building functional iPhone and iPad applications, be sure to check out the second part of this series, *iOS Succinctly*. This hands-on guide to app development applies all of the Objective-C skills acquired from this book to real-world development situations. We'll walk through all of the major Objective-C frameworks and learn how to perform tasks along the way, including: configuring user interfaces, capturing input, drawing graphics, saving and loading files, and much, much more.

www.ingramcontent.com/pod-product-compliance
Lightning Source LLC
Chambersburg PA
CBHW071257050326
40690CB00011B/2433